FINDING
A PLACE
TO SETTLE

THE BOOK OF RUTH: LEARNING TO FIND GOD-GIFTED IDENTITY

STEPHEN BISHOP

Zaccmedia

Published by Zaccmedia
www.zaccmedia.com
info@zaccmedia.com

Published May 2016

ISBN: 978-1-911211-24-2

British Library Cataloguing-in-Publication Data
A catalogue record for this book is available from the British Library.

CONTENTS

AUTHOR'S
NOTE

H is name was unfamiliar. It was also distinctly foreign. But as it was displayed on a Blue Plaque he must have been someone of note. However, as that plaque was situated on the wall of an ordinary terraced house – one of thousands – in east London, there was no clue as to the circumstances by which he had come to live there. So what had 'Solomon Plaatje, South African writer and campaigner for African rights,' been doing here, and who was he? Those brief details, together with the years of his birth and death, 1876–1932, did not give much away. The many curious glances of people who passed by and noticed the plaque indicated that I was not the only person who was bewildered!

Eventually I checked the details of Solomon Plaatje on the internet. The result was both fascinating and puzzling. It seems that his stay in Leyton, east London, would actually have been quite brief. He only visited London on three occasions, suggesting that he never put down roots in Britain even if that may have once have been his intention. This was because his focus was on his South African countrymen, their liberation and enfranchisement. In seeking to achieve those aims he was the founding member and first general secretary of what is now called the ANC (African National Congress).

But there was more. He was also a talented linguist who translated the works of Shakespeare into the Tswana language, something which I suspect not many people can claim to have achieved! He was a journalist and had been raised by Christian parents, also being educated by German missionaries. Finally it was also stressed that he was a committed Christian.

Although this information failed to fill some big gaps about the life of Solomon Plaatje, it was apparent that he eventually came to recognise the calling to which he needed to give himself. How and when this became clear is not recorded. Nor were details provided of those who influenced and supported him. Finally, and of particular interest to me, living in the same road where that plaque was displayed, the length of time that he spent in this part of London was not stated.

All that can be deduced from those brief website entries was that this man had been on a journey. It was clearly a geographic one, but more importantly it was also vocational and spiritual. And somewhere in the course of those travels he paused to spend time in a house on the outskirts of a big city.

This brief study is focused on Ruth, someone in the Bible who, as with Solomon Plaatje and, probably, ourselves, was not well known but on a spiritual journey. Like us, the circumstances and choices in her life were difficult but instrumental in shaping it. The unfolding events in the biblical book named after her not only showed God's intervention but also Him bringing her to a place of understanding her identity and calling.

So an invitation is part of the 'package' in this material! It's that we take time to pause and take stock of where and who we are in terms of our God-gifted identity. However long or short our journey with God, the opportunity to reflect on what He is also underlining for us can be a means, as with Ruth, in us finding a place to *'settle'*.

1

INTRODUCTION

LOSING OUR WAY

He led them by a straight way to a city
where they could settle.
(Psalm 107:7)

READ: PSALM 107

Technology now exists which means that no one should get lost... in theory! Sat Navs and GPS devices are designed so that motorists, cyclists and even pedestrians should not only be able to determine their current position but also be guided to a designated destination. Public transport, particularly buses and trains, also provide on-board travel information geared to ensure that passengers arrive at the right stopping-off point.

However, in practice things can work out very differently. Incorrect input data, unforeseen diversions, failure to follow directions and misreading information can all result in delays or disruption. A further factor can be assuming that transport systems are operating normally when, in fact, they are not. A part-closure of the London Underground network in a recent summer break caught out many travellers who only used that particular line occasionally. So system malfunction or human failings (or a combination) can contribute to unhappy or unsuccessful journey 'experiences'!

A SPIRITUAL JOURNEY

The writer of Psalm 107 would not have been familiar with modern technology but he recognised the importance of travelling safely to a specified destination... and the many factors that could prevent it. The problems arising in such a scenario were categorised in this psalm. But they did not only relate to purely physical circumstances or an actual point on the map. That's because the writer was illustrating different barriers encountered in our spiritual journey through life... and finding God's purposes for us. So the descriptions found here involved an interwoven element of physical, emotional and spiritual aspects.

The main picture was of the Children of Israel trekking through the desert on their way to the Promised Land with other 'sub-plots' thrown into the mix. The end result of their journey after overcoming obstacles was of people being led to *'a city where they could settle'* (verses 4,7,36).

It was only when arriving at their destination that the Children of Israel were in a place of growth and fulfilment. *'They sowed fields and planted vineyards that yielded a fruitful harvest; he blessed them, and their numbers greatly increased, and he did not let their herds diminish'* (verses 37,38). Whilst this picture of agricultural prosperity may not be applicable to ourselves, the picture it paints of thriving, flourishing and wholeness can be aspects of life to which we seriously aspire.

LIFE TO THE FULL

God created us to achieve those aspirations – to find our identity. His instruction to the first man set that objective: *'God blessed them and said to them, "Be fruitful and increase in number; fill the earth and subdue it. Rule over the fish of the sea and the birds of the air and over every living creature that moves on the ground"'* (Genesis 1:28). Jesus reaffirmed this when He stated: *'I have come that they may have life, and have it to the full'* (John 10:10). However, this was not to be carried out in isolation but in partnership with God. This 'working relationship' was to be enabled by having a personal and deepening bond with God as pictured in the Genesis account describing Him *'... walking in the garden in the cool of the day'* (3:8).

The problem that many people, even Christians, encounter in seeking to satisfy this need for fulfilment and fruitfulness is the same as subsequently described in Genesis. We view it in purely physical and material terms. God is pushed out of the equation and we try to achieve wholeness by means of personal ability and ingenuity.

God is pushed out of the equation...

We consequently fail badly in attaining what we want. In addition there are a multitude of factors (including other people!) that conspire against our efforts. It's not only 'ordinary' people who are thwarted. British prime minister Benjamin Disraeli was quoted as saying, 'I have climbed to the top of the greasy pole' when elected to office in 1868, indicating awareness of the temporary and precarious nature of success. Ruth in the Old Testament would have been viewed as a complete 'no-hoper' in achieving fulfilment and personal growth. Yet she took faltering steps alongside her mother-in-law, Naomi, to find such a place.

This drive for more, *'a city where they could settle'*, was therefore the starting point for the psalmist to describe various obstacles which prevented, or delayed, arrival at such a place. Five barriers were highlighted and each was to impinge upon Ruth, as with ourselves. So it's necessary to explore them as a backdrop against the account of Ruth as she embarked on her physical and spiritual journey.

WANDERING

The psalmist started off by describing the state of those who were undertaking this search for a city. They were recorded as those who *'wandered'* (verse 4). As a consequence they were in a *'desert wasteland'* where *'They were hungry and thirsty, and their lives ebbed away'* (verse 5). It is strange that this age could be similarly labelled. Education systems and employment structures are specifically geared to leading students and employees into areas of study and career development that optimise skills and qualifications. Advice also exists for positive 'work-life' balances to be attained. Yet many people exist on the basis of short-term, superficial or unachievable goals, if any at all. Lee Marvin sang many years ago about being born under a wandering star, and this seems to be a common unspoken mantra.

When the psalmist wrote *'I have strayed like a lost sheep'* (Psalm 119:176), he was not only describing the plight of those who had no relationship with God, but also those who once did. The prophet Isaiah summed this up by declaring: *'We all, like sheep, have gone astray, each of us has turned to his own way...'* (53:6). This was certainly true of the Children of Israel, whose 'wilderness wanderings' after their escape from Egypt resulted in what was essentially an eleven-day journey being extended to forty years – and not because of a faulty Sat Nav! Their disobedience and self-centredness resulted in drifting around a barren landscape suffering literal and spiritual hunger and thirst. In contrast, the psalmist described a committed focus upon God: *'Your face, LORD,*

I will seek' (Psalm 27:8). The outcome was completely different from that experienced by those Israelites: *'I am still confident of this: I will see the goodness of the LORD in the land of the living'* (Psalm 27:13). The spiritual environment in which Ruth and Naomi were living was one in which people were still generally pushing God away, resulting in aimlessness impacting these women's lives.

REBELLION

The second obstacle to achieving a place of real fulfilment recorded in Psalm 107 was rebellion against God and what He had said. Although this is similar to wandering from God, it indicated a deliberate refusal to follow His ways and direction. These were shared with the Israelites through His word. We are often oblivious to the power and importance of words. At one level they may simply seem to consist of physical interactions between our mouths, air waves, eardrums and intellect. But the Bible brings a very different scenario – words have power! A spiritual as well as physical dynamic is at work. This is particularly true of God. When He speaks then things happen – big time! God spoke this universe into being (see Genesis 1; Psalm 33:6). This world continues to exist because of God's word: *'The Son is the radiance of God's glory ... sustaining all things by his powerful word'* (Hebrews 1:3).

Specifically it is God's word which we need to hear and obey in order to experience life in all its fullness. The rebuke which Jesus directed at the devil when tempted were words originally spoken to the Israelites when in the desert: *'Man does not live on bread alone, but on every word that comes from the mouth of God'* (Matthew 4:4). The Old Testament passage preceded this declaration with a comparison of the Israelites being fed by God with *'manna'*, which was a means of teaching them to depend upon Him.

...find ourselves imprisoned in thought patterns...

Sadly the Israelites, alongside ourselves, listen to other words. These generate doubt, disbelief and denial. We can consequently find ourselves imprisoned in thought patterns that render us powerless in finding life as God intended. It was Jesus Himself who drew attention of the power of His words in bringing release: *'The words I have spoken to you are spirit and they are life'*; *'He has sent me to proclaim freedom for the prisoners...'* (John 6:63; Luke 4:18). The psalmist described it in this way: *'Then they cried to the LORD in their trouble, and he saved them from their distress. He brought them out of darkness and the deepest gloom'* (Psalm 107:13,14). In tracing Ruth's journey we will find that God's word through other people was instrumental in bringing life-giving change to her.

CROOKEDNESS

'Iniquities' are described as the third obstacle to experiencing God's provision of life in all its fullness. Although we may substitute the word 'sin', the original Hebrew word is derived from the one relating to 'bend' or 'distort'. It points to our crooked or warped behaviour patterns leading to rebellion against God. The consequences are described as affliction, distress and drawing near to *'the gates of death'*. This seemed to relate, in the immediate context, to physical well-being. Certainly a person's bodily health is closely related to the ability to thrive in other ways, such as intellectually, emotionally and even spiritually. This was why famine and drought were sent by God upon the Israelites. These were one way of bringing their attention to something being seriously wrong! It was a factor in the early stages of Ruth's life.

6

STORMS

The plight of those encountering fierce storms as they carried cargo on ships, the fourth element in this series of obstacles described in Psalm 107, suggested people who were self-reliant and self-confident. It would take a lot of both of these qualities to leave sight of land in the comparatively frail sailing craft of those days. Those who were prepared to take big risks (or even small ones) without any regard for God would find themselves 'at their wits' end' (verse 27). Whilst life is full of decisions and unknowns needing to be faced, leaving God out of the equation as did these sailors is not only unwise, but unsafe! Ruth's life was affected, again in the early stages, by people who had seemingly ignored God.

TURNING THEIR BACK

Finally, the picture of the Israelites having settled in the Promised Land but experiencing 'oppression, calamity and sorrow' (verse 39) could refer to God's people turning their back on Him when brought to a position of prosperity. Expulsion and exile was eventually inflicted upon them. This was followed, after a period, by restoration and a return to their homes when God's

...God's people responded to Him.

people responded to Him. Even in a place of blessing and fruitfulness there needs to be an ongoing God-awareness, an acknowledgement that He is the source of life and flourishing. The prophet wrote of God underlining this: '... your fruitfulness comes from me' (Hosea 14:8). Ruth continued to look to God even in adverse and uncertain circumstances. It enabled her to move into the purposes of God for her life and a place where she could 'settle'.

The psalmist had started by describing God as the One who *'redeemed'*. This was particularly important in the account of Ruth, as we shall see. She was eventually brought to find her uniqueness and significance through the human agency of a 'kinsman-redeemer', someone who was representative of Jesus, accepting her and providing security. These are needs which God wants to meet in our lives as well – that we also might be brought to a place where we can *'settle'*.

FOR REFLECTION

1. Why can the term 'spiritual journey' (or 'faith journey') be helpful in assessing our relationship with God?

2. Which of the five spiritual scenarios described in Psalm 107 most closely matches where you are in spiritual terms, and why?

3. The writer encourages us to note what's been described in this psalm (verse 43). Why do you feel that this is important?

4. God is described as bringing people to a place where *'they could settle'* (verse 4). What value is there in being in such a place, and how do you feel this can work out in practical ways today?

2

OUT OF
CONTROL

*... and a man from Bethlehem in Judah, together with his wife and two
sons, went to live for a while in the country of Moab.*
(Ruth 1:1)

READ: RUTH 1:1,2

People, it seems, are always on the move. London has its 8 million
residents swelled almost daily by thousands of tourists and
visitors. In addition there are swarms of commuters who travel
from outlying areas – some over two hours' travelling time – to
work in or around the city. To these are added increasing numbers
from overseas who chose to migrate to this huge conurbation.
They have contributed to the cosmopolitan flavour of the streets
and communities where they have settled. Alongside my own
house are homes where families from India, Pakistan, Lithuania,
Poland, Somalia and the Caribbean have put down roots. Many
reasons arise for such migration to take place. At least some has
been on account of adverse pressures in their country of origin.

So it is not surprising to read of similar population movements
recorded in the Bible. Jesus, even as an unborn baby, was caught

up in this scenario. His mother and her husband were forced to trek many miles on account of an official edict. But our particular story steps back even earlier in time. Bethlehem, however, was still the common factor. On this occasion, instead of Joseph and the pregnant Mary trudging up the road leading into the town, we see a man and his small family heading in the opposite direction, out of it. Neither event made an impression upon onlookers since neither family had any status. Like others, they were just part of the jetsam and flotsam of humanity caught up in circumstances outside of their control, having little or no choice as to how to respond.

POLITICS AND ECONOMICS

For Joseph and Mary, their journey into Bethlehem arose out of living in a corner of the far-flung Roman Empire, whose authoritarian leader ordered the registration of his subjects. This was purely for tax revenue purposes. A similar mixture of politics and economics was forcing a man to take his family away. The opening sentence of this book of Ruth points to the former. *'In the days when the judges ruled...'* (1:1) This was a time following the leadership of Joshua and the elders who succeeded him. The Israelites had escaped from slavery in Egypt and been led through the wilderness before entering the land that God had promised to give them. Many years of ongoing military action against the inhabitants of the land ended with the different tribal groups being allocated specific geographical areas within its boundaries.

Although God's people were now settled in their new territory, they failed to be settled in their commitment to God – not a good idea! They adopted the idolatry and pagan practices of the previous occupants and seemed oblivious to possible consequences. Although severely warned by Joshua of the need to wholly follow God and His ways, with his death and then the elders who outlived him, the people moved away from God. Their wilderness wanderings may have ceased many years before, but wandering in a spiritual sense continued.

THE JUDGES

God was neither ignorant nor inactive with regard to this waywardness by His people. He allowed their enemies to invade and oppress them. A cycle developed whereby they would cry to God in response to such affliction and He would then raise up a leader to free them. These men (and, at one time, a woman) were called Judges, the Old Testament narrative recording their exploits in the book of that name.

Verses in an early chapter of the book of Judges set the scene: *'Whenever the LORD raised up a judge for them, he was with the judge and saved them out of the hands of their enemies as long as the judge lived; for the LORD had compassion on them as they groaned under those who oppressed and afflicted them. But when the judge died, the people returned to ways even more corrupt then those of their fathers … They refused to give up their evil practices and stubborn ways'* (Judges 2:18,19).[1]

Some of these judges were exercising their God-given authority for many years and in a national capacity. Others may have been used by God for a comparatively shorter length of time, and in a relatively smaller geographical area. But the whole atmosphere of this period, reckoned to be from 1380 to 1050 BC, was one of uncertainty, upheaval and instability. The moral and spiritual inconsistency of those days had a knock-on effect in the political arena that is best summed up by the last words of that book:

1   For a fuller description of this era the book *Fleeces, Fears and Flames* by the same author may be helpful (Zaccmedia, 2014).

'In those days Israel had no king; everyone did as he saw fit' (Judges 21:25); *'... every man did that which was right in his own eyes'* KJV).

FAMINE

But there was another factor to be thrown into this mix. *'... there was a famine in the land'* (1:1). No other details were provided and there was no direct reference to such an event in the book of Judges. It could have been a fairly localised episode or may have been widespread. Certainly the events leading up to the call of Gideon as Judge suggest that food shortages were a major driver in causing the Israelites to turn back to God when He allowed incursions by their enemies. *'Again the Israelites did evil in the eyes of the LORD, and for seven years he gave them into the hands of the Midianites ... Whenever the Israelites planted their crops, the Midianites, Amalekites and other eastern peoples invaded the country. They ... ruined the crops all the way to Gaza and did not spare a living thing for Israel, neither sheep nor cattle nor donkeys'* (Judges 6:1,3,4).

Years before this series of devastating events Moses, their great leader, had issued clear warnings that disobedience to God would result in severe discipline. This would involve scorching heat, drought, blight and mildew. Such cursing would also cause the sky to become *'bronze'* and the ground, *'iron'*, with the country becoming *'dust'* and *'powder'* (see Deuteronomy 28). Whatever the immediate cause of famine, whether enemy activity, ecological effects, or direct divine intervention, this whole situation was not good news! The population was entirely dependent upon agriculture to sustain life and produce some form of income. Land stewardship was an essential feature of life at this time. This was why each tribal group of the Children

...this whole situation was not good news!

of Israel had specific territorial boundaries, with clans and families within them being given parcels of land.

THE ROAD TO MOAB

Elimelech, as husband and father, was not only described in these opening verses of the book of Ruth as making a choice to leave his country and home town, but also seemingly to abandon the tract of land on which his family's livelihood had depended. What may therefore be regarded as a bad decision was then compounded by the direction of the road that he then led his family. They were heading towards Moab and away from Bethlehem, a name which meant, ironically, 'House of bread'.

This destination may have met their needs for food, but little else. Located on the eastern borders of Israel, there was ongoing friction between these two neighbouring states. The people of Moab were descended from the son of Lot (the nephew of Abraham) and his older daughter who committed incest following their dramatic escape from the annihilation of Sodom and Gomorrah, Lot's daughters being fearful that there would be no continuation of their family line. It was the king of Moab who had subsequently and unsuccessfully attempted to bring down spiritual curses upon the Israelites when undertaking the last stage of their journey to the Promised Land. However, he was successful in his later ploy of seducing them into immorality, which resulted in God's response of severe discipline (see Numbers 25).[2]

DESPERATION

So this little family was figuratively and literally stepping into an unhealthy environment. Their lives were out of control, as were

---

2   See also *Dialogue With a Donkey* by the same author (Zaccmedia, 2014).

...familiar sights and sounds... gradually disappeared...

the circumstances around them. We are not told the feelings that were being experienced by Elimelech and Naomi, his wife. We can only conjecture their sense of helplessness, bewilderment and desperation as the familiar sights and sounds of their home town gradually disappeared behind their backs.

Whilst we may be spared the extremity of food shortages or other essentials being absent, there may still be situations which generate similar feelings. Circumstances outside of our control, such as redundancy, zero-hours contracts, rising housing costs, government spending cuts, family pressures and health issues are amongst the many factors that can deeply affect us... and force us to make choices that are not only unwise but appear unavoidable. As with Naomi, the knock-on effect with regard to our sense of identity may not be immediately obvious, but can be very profound.

Sadly the journey for Elimelech's family, including Naomi, who was to be ever-present in this unfolding story, had not ended even when they had arrived in Moab. They may had found food, but further loss in this horrific uncontrolled roller coaster of events was to be experienced.

FOR REFLECTION

1. Elimelech was preoccupied with famine. What adverse issues affect you?

2. Why do you think that Elimelech made no apparent reference to God when deciding to leave Bethlehem?

3. Why is it difficult to focus on God when facing adverse circumstances?

4. What do you think Naomi felt about this whole situation?

5. How much do you identify with being caught up in uncontrollable circumstances?

3

WHEN THE BOTTOM DROPS OUT

After they had lived there about ten years, both Mahlon and Kilion also died, and Naomi was left without her two sons and her husband.
(Ruth 1:4,5)

READ RUTH 1:,3-5

The haunting picture of an Italian policeman standing on a beach holding the lifeless body of a young child hit the media front pages in an astounding way. People who may have been previously oblivious to the plight of migrants seeking sanctuary in Europe from the horrors of life in North Africa and having to undertake a perilous sea voyage with the threat of drowning were now confronted with the grim truth. This 2015 tragedy underlined that escaping from one fear did not mean that trouble was now a thing of the past.

The choice that Elimelech had made to migrate with his family away from their home and country may have seemed the only option open to him. Circumstances beyond his control by way of famine had forced him to travel to neighbouring Moab in order to find food. His intention was, it appeared, to stay there only *'for a while'* (1:1). However, at no point was there any suggestion that Elimelech had turned to God or asked for His guidance and help. This omission was all the more poignant when considering his name, which meant, 'God is King'.

SPOTLIGHT ON NAOMI

Elimelech's failure to go to God was compounded, as far as his wife and two sons were concerned, when he died. The biblical account is silent regarding the timing or cause of his death. What did happen, however, was to move the spotlight onto Naomi, his widow. Although her reaction to this bereavement was not described at this point, her subsequent comment about her life being made *'bitter'* (1:20) indicated that this loss was a deep blow. The writer of the Proverbs brought the following perspective: *'Each heart knows its own bitterness, and no-one else can share its joy'* (Proverbs 14:10).

Loss can entail a whole raft of feelings pounding upon us, such as abandonment, rejection, separation, despair, emptiness and hopelessness. Contrary to popular thought, time does not bring healing. It never can. Many of us have experienced loss in this way and know that scars and memories will remain. Naomi's grief simply mirrored the stark realities of life which we all face.

WIDOWED AND CHILDLESS

However, Naomi's situation was to deteriorate more. The bottom was about to drop out of her world. Her two sons, now fatherless, had grown up and married women from Moab. Although this was not forbidden for Israelites, the Levitical law decreed that no Moabite or his sons to the tenth generation was allowed to enter *'the assembly of the LORD'* (Deuteronomy 23:3). How Naomi's two sons had ended up in such marriages was, again, not described.

Although it seemed that their culture provided for 'arranged' marriages, this was not automatically adopted. Isaac, the patriarch, had an older son named Esau whose choice of wives was entirely his own and were a source of grief to his parents on account of them being foreign (see Genesis 26:34,35). Perhaps the ongoing famine in Naomi's home town prevented a return for the purpose of finding a wife for each of these sons. This left the only alternative of marrying local girls whose spiritual background was distinctly anti-God. To Naomi's spiritually sensitive heart, such a step must have been hard to bear, since any resultant offspring were inevitably going to be raised in an alien environment.

However, this scenario became irrelevant when a final tragedy befell Naomi. Having lived in Moab for about ten years her two sons also died. Moreover, neither son had any children. This meant that Naomi was both a widow and childless. Being away from friends and any remaining, though distant, family members and in a foreign culture cut off from any supporting network derived from her faith, her deep grief and desolation can only be imagined. Added to this profound abandonment must have been a feeling of extreme hopelessness. As a woman and a widow with no supporting grandchildren or, it seems, close relatives, she had no one to care for her and no means of livelihood in the male-dominated society of her times.

> …a feeling of extreme hopelessness.

BEREAVEMENT

Although the term 'bereavement' does not appear in the Bible, the effects and feelings which stem from it are clearly described. Words such as afflicted, anguish, cut off, loss of hope and a general sense of destitution are often used. Jeremiah the prophet described the effects of desolation in the book of Lamentations, identifying with the heart-rending horrors being exacted upon his countrymen by God. *'I am the man who has seen affliction by the rod of his wrath. He has driven me away and made me walk in darkness rather than light; indeed, he has turned his hand against me again and again, all day long ... I remember my affliction and my wandering, the bitterness and the gall. I well remember them, and my soul is downcast within me'* (Lamentations 3:1–3,19,20).

Similarly the psalmist wrote of feeling deeply abandoned: *'Turn to me and be gracious to me, for I am lonely and afflicted. The troubles of my heart have multiplied; free me from my anguish. Look upon my affliction and my distress and take away all my sins. See how my enemies have increased and how fiercely they hate me!'* (Psalm 25:16–19).

NO TEARS LEFT

Unlike the reactions from these Old Testament writers, the response of Naomi to these successive blows is not immediately described. Nor does she indicate how she felt about God. Perhaps the culmination of these events was so great that she was simply incapable of connecting with her feelings or expressing them in words. Indeed, there are occasions when language is simply inadequate. Tears are the only outlet. We read that even Jesus *'wept'* (John 11:35), arising from the news of His friend, Lazarus, dying. Again, the psalmist could not find words to convey his grief and emptiness when under pressure: *'My tears have been my food day and night...'* (Psalm 42:3). And King David's spiritual 'vocabulary' made use of weeping, since he once asked God to *'Record my lament; list my tears on your scroll'* (Psalm 56:8). Another woman, Hannah, was also to experience anguish and hopelessness to the extent that tears were her only response to childlessness and shame.

But perhaps Naomi had no tears left to shed. The disaster of famine at home, the enforced trek away from friends, family, community and allotted tract of land, together with having to live in an alien environment, had possibly exhausted Naomi's supply of emotional response over the many years that had now passed.

IDENTITY

This bereavement also had a deep impact on her identity, as it will do on our own, though not necessarily in the same way. Although not quantifiable or easily assessed, her significance in the community was now reduced on account of being a childless widow. Her uniqueness was no longer so apparent, since those closest to her in reflecting this specialness were now dead. As a result, her purpose, particularly evident in being a wife and mother (and potential grandmother) no longer existed.

Naomi's emotional and spiritual state paint a bleak picture. But was she alone in having these experiences, the only person who had to bear such grief? The answer is that Jesus, the Son of God, experienced the fullest depth and weight of bereavement and grief. These caused Him to offer up *'loud cries and tears'* Hebrews 5:7) to His heavenly Father at both Gethsemane and Calvary. These places revealed the extent of His desolation and abandonment. As a result, we have One who is fully able to *'sympathise with our weaknesses'* (Hebrew 4:15).

Somewhere in the background of all of Naomi's intense suffering, God was both watching... and caring. He was also about to act in a clear way, **...God was both watching...and caring.** having previously been present in those dark shadows of her life. All the time God was identifying with Naomi's deep hurt, as the prophet described in the following way: *'In all their distress he too was distressed'* (Isaiah 63:9).

When our lives have taken directions that we neither planned nor expected, and when the bottom drops out, God is somehow still present with us. This is even when the tears of grief, loss and despair flow in response to the darkness and pressures that we experience. God is there to share in our griefs and sorrows, understanding all that is going on within us at the deepest level... and able to bring change, as Naomi was about to discover.

FOR REFLECTION

1. What kind of practical and emotional support do you think Naomi might have received had she still been in Bethlehem when bereaved?
2. What is the value of being alongside other people who are sharing in the same bereavement?
3. Why are tears so important?
4. What can be some of the effects on our identity (our uniqueness, significance and purpose) when suffering bereavement?

4

RETRACED STEPS

"When she head in Moab that the LORD had come to the aid of his people by providing food for them, Naomi and her daughters-in-law prepared to return home from there."
(Ruth 1:6)

READ: RUTH 1:6,7

We are back on that road again. This was the one that, many years previously, Naomi had travelled as a wife and mother. The lack of food had driven her family into an alien country, away from their home in Bethlehem, part of the tribal area of Judah. Now she is described as returning home. But there is a poignant difference as she prepares to retrace her steps. She is now a childless widow, alone apart from her daughters-in-law who did not share her godly background and upbringing.

OTHERS ON THIS JOURNEY

As we picture this older woman returning home, we need to understand that hers is not a unique journey. Others, before and afterwards, have had to travel a similar road, not so much geographical as spiritual. Even the great patriarch Abraham had to trek back the way that he'd come after going down to Egypt on account of a famine being experienced in the land to which God had called him (see Genesis 12:10–13:1). Joseph, Abraham's great-grandson, also went down to Egypt. This was not out of choice – he was a slave! Nevertheless, he knew that the Promised Land was his real home in spiritual terms, and therefore gave instructions about his bones being brought back on that same route that he had been taken when alive (see Hebrews 11:22). The Children of Israel's exodus from Egyptian slavery necessitated them retracing the steps of their forefathers taken those four centuries before.

The Promised Land was the God-given home for His people, even though their repeated failure to follow Him resulted in expulsion and forced exile. God's heart was for their return and restoration. The prophet Isaiah wrote of God's plan involving their steps being retraced: *'I will lead the blind by ways they have not known, along unfamiliar paths I will guide them; I will turn the darkness into light before them and make the rough places smooth. These are the things I will do; I will not forsake them'* (Isaiah 42:16).

A PROPHET AND A PARABLE

The prophet Jonah also had to retrace his steps. Being instructed by God to go to Ninevah and *'preach against it'* (Jonah 1:2) he unwisely turned and went in the opposite direction. Being swallowed by a *'great fish'* (1:17) after encountering a fierce storm and thrown overboard from the boat on which he was sailing, he recognised the need to do what he was told! So when vomited out onto dry land he took the initially required road to the city. Although a parable, Jesus' account of the prodigal son was another reminder of God's ways requiring us to have a change of heart and take the road back.

READINESS TO LISTEN

Naomi's own journey back home was not undertaken without specific elements being brought into place. The first of these was that she 'heard in Moab that the LORD had come to the aid of his people' (1:6). Events outside her control had severely battered and bruised her both emotionally and spiritually, bringing a sense of darkness and abandonment. Yet she was still ready to hear about God and respond positively to what He was doing.

Such a reaction was not to be taken for granted. Sadly, there are huge numbers of people in this world who find themselves the victims of atrocities and tragedies completely outside of their control. Their reaction has been to reject God. *Why Do Bad Things Happen to Good People?* (Anchor, 2004) was the title of Rabi Harold S. Kushner's book, written whilst trying to grapple with suffering and the omniscience of God.

But Naomi chose not to respond by pushing away a belief in God's control and love. She did not discard, reject or ridicule this news about the provision of food. It is also important to notice that she was hearing about God even though she was in Moab, an environment

...she was hearing about God...

where God was not honoured or readily followed. This was not a place where people were encouraged to hear God. But even in the spiritually darkest and distant places we can listen and respond to God – Jonah in that fish is further evidence to that fact!

GOD'S INTERVENTION

It is clear that Naomi, hearing of food now being available back home, accepted this fact as being the result of God's intervention. This was the second important element of her decision to return to Bethlehem. She did not view this situation as being a coincidence, 'one of those things', an accident or a 'natural' event. She saw this provision as being the specific work of God. He was involved in what was taking place. This was not going to be an isolated example of her attitude towards God. It showed that she believed in the reality of God being the One who worked in this world, and who continued to do so. This was to be epitomised and wonderfully evidenced in the coming of Jesus many centuries later: '*Immanuel – which means, "God with us"*' (Matthew 1:23).

OPPORTUNITY

Naomi's response was also one which illustrated her sensitivity in recognising and seizing opportunity. This third element that contributed to her retracing her steps indicated a readiness to take a big risk. However remote it might have been, she nevertheless saw this news as a chance to see her life put back together.

There was no indication that the food shortage had ended earlier – this was the first time that it was recorded that there had been a change in the situation. Naomi was in a state of mind and heart, however tentatively, to pick up on this development. *Carpe diem* – 'seize the day' could have been her motivation! Again this was not going to be the only occasion in her life when she discerned the possibility of something being different and took hold of an opportunity. Admittedly she did not feel that she had anything going for her. Subsequent comments when she actually arrived home were to reveal that feeling. But what she did have, despite the horrific turmoil arising from her experiences, was an unstated but resolute belief in God being present and active. Her willingness to step out (literally and spiritually) in the light of this change of circumstances with the opportunity that it presented was based on this trust.

PREPARATION

The fourth element in undertaking this journey was that she *'prepared to return ... from there'* (1:6). This indicated that the decision was not an impetuous, spur of the moment, knee-jerk reaction. Preparation meant pausing to think through what was happening, considering her current situation and possible consequences once she had arrived back in Bethlehem. As with these other elements, preparation was to be an aspect of her life which would feature again in an even more important context. But it showed that she was willing to stop and think.

Whilst God has created us as spiritual beings, part of this 'package' is the ability to work things through with our minds. The latter are to be transformed and renewed into line with God's good, pleasing and perfect will (see Romans 12:2). Whilst the heart, the source of our emotions and will is made 'new' by God's Spirit, we have the responsibility to work with God on our thought-life and thinking processes.

SENSITIVITY

Somehow, in all the events of those more recent years, Naomi's heart and mind had remained open to God. Her response to adversity could have been very different. But it was her sensitivity – and associated submissiveness – to God in all that was going on around and within her that enabled her to perceive God's hand in the lifting of the famine and then preparing to return home. This was the next element which enabled her to act.

That word 'submissiveness' is not reckoned as being politically correct in today's environment, nor necessarily in church circles. Yet our submission to God's work and ways in our lives, followed by submission to others, can be key to experiencing opportunities that He opens up for us. It is definitely integral to combat spiritual and worldly influences (see James 4:7; Ephesians 5:21).

At no point had we read that Naomi had argued the case against leaving Bethlehem when her husband decided to move away, or contended with her sons when they opted to marry girls from Moab, or acted to return home prematurely. In maintaining that submissive attitude she found herself in the right spiritual place to move on and retrace her steps when the opportunity arose.

SEVERING TIES

Finally Naomi was ready to leave the place where she had been living. There may have been strong emotional ties to that place on account of it being where she had last seen her husband and sons alive. She may have put down roots which now had to be taken up again.

> ...the call of God in her life...

But she was finding that the call of God in her life, however faint at this stage, demanded that she make this move. Perhaps it was for the sake of her two daughters-in-law that she had decided to stay put after the death of her sons, their husbands. She had experienced the grief in losing a spouse and possibly felt the need to remain alongside those girls as they tried to piece their lives, including their childlessness, back together.

Naomi had shown that she was not one to 'up and off' at the slightest hint as seems to be the case in today's society, where it is reckoned that people move house an average of eight times in their lives. But when a call of God is sensed then there needs to be a response. When God called the Israelites to leave their familiar surroundings in exile, He directed them to: *'Forget the former things; do not dwell on the past. See, I am doing a new thing! Now it springs up; do you not perceive it? I am making a way in the desert and streams in the wasteland'* (Isaiah 43:18,19).

RECOGNITION

Naomi, in believing that the news about the famine in her home country being ended was an indication to return, showed a sensitivity that we also need to nurture. She recognised that, however faint, this was a call from God. Those were not just tangible and obvious outward circumstances that she identified. She was sensitive to the possibility of change being brought by God. Having such openness to Him even in the adversity is often the road to a greater experience of God at work, as Naomi was to find including restoration of her identity.

FOR REFLECTION

1. Why is it important to hang on to a belief in God and His character even in adversity?
2. Why is 'stepping out' ('seizing the day') a necessary part of our relationship with God?
3. How do you think that submissiveness can bring about a greater degree of sensitivity to God?
4. In what ways have you felt God speak to you about retracing your steps?

5

HOLDING ON

But Ruth replied, 'Don't urge me to leave you or to turn back from
you. Where you go I will go, and where you stay I will stay.
Your people will be my people and your God my God.'
(Ruth 1:16)

READ: RUTH 1:8-18

Just as Naomi had been a distant figure in the opening verses of
this book, so Ruth had not been described in any detail. She had
simply been a Moabite woman who had married one of Naomi's
sons prior to herself then being widowed. But she was now about
to take centre stage. As she does so, we find that her feelings and
thinking have been drastically realigned.

Such a shift in Ruth's focus became evident after a long period
of time. This was no sudden decision, spur-of-the-moment choice,
or even a 'Damascus Road'-type conversion. Ruth's perspective
had been changing over many years. Her husband had married
her and lived in Moab for *'about ten years'* (1:4) before he had died.
Then after an unstated duration Naomi had heard the news of
God coming to the aid of His people who had previously been
suffering famine conditions. It does not seem that Naomi had

necessarily left Moab straight away to return home in response to this news.

Throughout this period of marriage, bereavement and then Naomi's reassessment of her situation, Ruth was in the background. She was watching, learning, absorbing and sensing what her mother-in-law was going through and, undoubtedly, interacting with her. Time was a vital factor for Ruth to process within herself the feelings and beliefs that were being observed in this older woman.

WAITING

This element of time and handling what was taking place contrasts with our own 'instant' age. Information technology means that we now receive communications in milliseconds and are required to respond or act within moments. Speed dating, text messaging, contactless card payments are just a few symptoms of this 'now' culture which cannot seem to wait. Which is unfortunate... because God is not in a hurry! It's part of His style, being patient and working in our lives step by step so that we trust Him even through seasons of 'waiting' when nothing seems to be happening.

God Himself waited until the right time had come before sending His Son into this world. Jesus' ministry only began after having waited for thirty years of preparation to be completed. He was in the tomb for three days before He was resurrected from the dead. Another forty days passed before He ascended to heaven. Then the disciples had to wait for the Day of Pentecost before being filled with God's Holy Spirit. 'Time' is a means by which God choses to work in this world and in our lives. It is not wasted if we respond to what He is doing. It is a process that cannot be condensed or bypassed.

RUTH'S DECLARATION

What was Ruth sensing and learning during those many years of being around Naomi? Whatever it was, it made a profound impact. It was evidenced when Ruth made that amazing declaration: *'Where you go I will go, and where you stay I will stay. Your people will be my people and your God my God. Where you die I will die, and there will I be buried. May the* LORD *deal with me, be it ever so severely, if anything but death separates you and me'* (1:16,17). The force of these words is underlined when considering the response of her sister-in-law, Orpah. She had also, presumably, observed Naomi when sustaining succeeding emotional and spiritual blows. But her steps were in the opposite direction: *'Then Orpah kissed her mother-in-law goodbye...'* (1:14).

In contrast, the heart-response of Ruth to Naomi was that she *'clung'* (1:14) to her. There are, perhaps, three aspects of Naomi's life which caused Ruth to commit herself to a dramatically different direction in life from that of her sister-in-law and her upbringing. The first of these was that Naomi faced up to reality – she was 'real' about what was taking place. She was also realistic about future prospects. When her daughters-in-law told her that they would stay with her when she returned to her own people, Naomi was brutally frank: *'Why would you come with me? Am I going to have any more sons, who could become your husbands? Return home, my daughters; I am too old to have another husband. Even if I thought there was still hope for me – even if I had a husband tonight and then gave birth to sons – would you wait until they grew up? Would you remain unmarried for them?'* (1:11–13).

...she was 'real' about what was taking place.

33

BEING 'UPFRONT'

It is neither godly nor wise to bury our heads in the sand, brush situations under the carpet, be in a state of denial, or pretend that things are different. It is noticeable that Jeremiah, the Old Testament prophet, only came to realise the hope of God's goodness and faithfulness subsequent to confronting and expressing his list of very real troubles (see Lamentations 3). Naomi's willingness to be real also extended to describing her feelings about God – which were far from positive: '... *the LORD's hand has gone out against me!*' (1:13) In that respect the psalmist comes alongside this distraught woman with some equally devastating details of his view of God. Psalm 13 raises some serious doubts about God's care and power: '*How long, O LORD? Will you forget me for ever? How long will you hide your face from me?*' (verse 1). But that's sometimes what it means to be real.

We may be able to hide from other people by wearing 'masks' of self-sufficiency, a sense of being able to hold things together, and not being fazed. But God sees below the surface of our lives. He is aware of our true condition and feelings. So we may as well be 'upfront' with Him and ourselves. Whatever the issues of life, especially those which were pressing in upon Naomi and Ruth such as relationships, loss, rejection, singleness, loneliness and childlessness, we need to be honest about them.

LETTING GO

The second element of Naomi's life which impacted Ruth was her willingness to let go. She had no presumptions regarding her two daughters-in-law and made no demands upon them. There were no expectations in respect of them accompanying her back home. As we have seen, she did the exact opposite, doing her best to dissuade them from going with her to Bethlehem when they had indicated that they would do so. *'No, my daughters'* (1:13) was her conclusion in responding to their plea to come with her. This was followed by a rebuff aimed specifically at Ruth after Orpah had turned back: *'"Look," said Naomi, "your sister-in-law is going back to her people and her gods. Go back with her"'* (1:15). Naomi persisted in attempting to dissuade Ruth even when the latter *'clung'* to her. The narrative concludes: *'When Naomi realised that Ruth was determined to go with her, she stopped urging her'* (1:18).

Whilst this description of that emotional scene showed Ruth's resolve, it also highlights Naomi's open-hearted nature. She refused to exercise any kind of control or manipulative behaviour towards other people. Again this seems to be very different from current thinking in which human rights, contractual obligations, responsibilities and back-up litigation are much in vogue. In contrast God speaks about love. The apostle Paul brings this into a practical setting when writing to the Christians in Rome: *'Let no debt remain outstanding, except the continuing debt to love one another, for he who loves his fellow-man has fulfilled the law'* (13:8). The well-known inspirational words of Paul (1 Corinthians 13) bring an awesome perspective to this attitude.

Even though Naomi's actions and words towards Ruth at this point seemed to be negative, they were actually displaying love that refused to place her daughter-in-law under any kind of duress. Clearer evidence of this deep concern was to be shown in subsequent events, but that could only come about after initial willingness to let go of Ruth and allow her to choose to return to her natural family and culture.

CLINGING TO GOD

If Naomi's attitude towards Ruth was one of readiness to let go, then the third aspect of her life that would have had a profound effect was her refusal to push God away. There are seven specific uses of the name 'LORD' (being the name used to denote the Lord God – Yahweh) in this opening chapter. Six of them are spoken by Naomi in the course of conversation, the last of these when she had arrived back in Bethlehem. But the first occasion of God's name being used by her was when talking to her daughters-in-law and urging them to return to their home: *"May the LORD show kindness to you, as you have shown to your dead and to me' (1:8)'"*. This would not appear to have been a glib or throwaway remark. The atmosphere in which this was said was full of emotion – Naomi's words came from the depth of her being and revealed a real awareness of God and His desire to intervene in people's lives.

These references can only provide a flavour of Naomi's relationship with God and her ongoing trust in Him which somehow sustained her, despite the harsh experiences that she had to endure. It clearly made a significant impression upon Ruth, because in confirming her desire to remain alongside she specifically highlighted Naomi's God being *'my God'* and her people as *'my people'* (1:16). Ruth was prepared to leave the many aspects of life that contributed to her own security and identity – familiar surroundings, family, friends and the culture of her birth – in order to stay with her mother-in-law. It was Naomi's deep conviction in the power and intervention of God – whatever her outward circumstances – that led Ruth to cling to her before subsequently being touched by God Himself in an unforeseen and wonderful way.

FOR REFLECTION

1. Why is it important to be 'real' with God about our adverse experiences?

2. In what ways can 'letting go' of legitimate demands and expectations contribute towards something that is positive? Read 1 Corinthians 13 in considering this question.

3. What makes it hard to keep trusting in God when things are not working out?

4. Ruth made a decision to stay with Naomi and leave many aspects of life that contributed towards her significance and specialness. What could be the equivalent aspects of life around us?

6

RUNNING
ON EMPTY

*So Naomi returned from Moab accompanied by Ruth the Moabitess,
her daughter-in-law, arriving in Bethlehem as the barley
harvest was beginning.*
(Ruth 1:22)

READ: RUTH 1: 19-22:

Naomi's return to her home in Bethlehem after being away for
many years might have been expected to be a joyous event. She
was coming back to relatives and a community to whom she
belonged, to a culture where she had been brought up, and to
a spiritual environment in which the life-giving presence of the
true God was acknowledged at least in part.

But the reactions of those living there, and of Naomi herself,
did not align with this positive expectation. Her arrival home
caused everyone to be *'stirred'* and women, particularly, to ask,
'Can this be Naomi?' The King James Version of the Bible describes
it in terms that *'... all the city was moved about them, and they said,
Is this Naomi?'* (1:19). The narrative also included the fact that she
was accompanied by Ruth, her daughter-in-law, clearly marking
her out as being *'the Moabitess'* (1:22).

GOING THROUGH THE MOTIONS

However, it is Naomi who is the focus of attention when arriving home. A phrase which could well be applied to her in the light of how she was about to describe herself was that she was 'running on empty'. Her emotional, mental and spiritual state were at a very low ebb. The term relates to the performance of tasks for which there is little, or no, energy left to actually undertake them. The motivation to take action is no longer present – the person could be said to be 'going through the motions'. Allied to this, the prospect of any change or improvement is excluded. Instead, there is the sense of despondency, hopelessness and negativity mixed in with all these other factors.

Athletes, particularly distance runners, use the term 'hitting the wall' to describe a similar scenario after having run a considerable time already and then coming to the end of their strength. The advice from sports trainers is to keep going until a further reserve of energy kicks in. My own experience is that as the years progress this so-called 'reserve' takes longer to access and seems to be of only short-term benefit!

NOTHING LEFT

Naomi had no such resources to enable her to break through. They had probably been exhausted years before when needing to cope with the devastating deaths, first of her husband, and then her two sons. Whatever emotional and mental energy and resolve that might have remained had now been channelled into getting her back to Bethlehem. That was as far as she could go. She had been running on empty. Now there was nothing left.

Many of us can identify with Naomi in this way. Whilst our outward circumstances may be very different, the draining of hope, aspiration, faith and love arising from so many possible demands can result in a sense of emptiness and a place of darkness. Naomi's statement in response to those who greeted her was a clear indication of this inner condition. She picked up on the question that was being asked, *'Can this be Naomi?'* and answered it with a despondent reply. She told them not to call her *'Naomi'* (her name meaning 'pleasant') but instead to call her *'Mara'* (which meant 'bitter'). This was because *'the Almighty has made my life very bitter'*. She elaborated: *'I went away full, but the* LORD *has brought me back empty'* (1:20,21).

GOD'S WAYS

At one level, Naomi was correct in her assessment. The loss of her husband and family had meant that she was alone and, particularly in the culture of her day, totally destitute. Her family line and the genealogy of which it was part – an essential element of her identity – had now ceased. It was also appropriate for her to bring God into the picture, doing so in very stark terms: *'The* LORD *has afflicted me; the Almighty has brought misfortune upon me'* (1:21). But was she making a valid statement? Was God directly, or indirectly, responsible for her suffering that she had endured, along with the consequences? Naomi's words may not sit easily with some Christians; the activity of God in this way does not seem to line up with His character as revealed in the Bible. This extremely sensitive area that impacts all of us in some way during our lives has demanded answers that many sincere Christians have tried to provide.

It can only be acknowledged that in all the attempts to reconcile pain and God's character, His ways and perspective are ultimately higher and different from our own. At the beginning of the last century an emerging, English preacher, Stuart Holden, received an invitation to speak in the USA. He believed that this was God's way ahead and accepted, making arrangements to travel across the Atlantic Ocean by ship since air transport did not exist at that time. However, his wife became ill and, no doubt reluctantly, he had to cancel this chance to expand his God-given preaching ministry on account of needing to care for his spouse. That may have seemed a hugely disappointing lost opportunity, except for one fact. The ship for which he had booked his passage (now cancelled) was... the RMS *Titanic*! Perhaps we are too quick to judge the hard situations that we encounter, and rule out God's ways of working in them.

> ...too quick to judge the hard situations...

NOT ALONE

This was the point to which Naomi needed to get. She may have come home in a physical and geographical sense, but spiritually she was still on a journey, including trying to find significance and specialness – her identity – alongside most of us! That's because although she had a picture of herself as being '*empty*', it was not her true position. She was neither empty nor alone. She had been accompanied by Ruth, '*the Moabitess*'. This was a simple yet profound statement, of vital importance.

God had worked through all of Naomi's years of emotional and spiritual turmoil and uncertainty, to touch the depths of another person. Ruth, someone from an anonymous background and an anti-God environment, with no pedigree or status, with nothing to make her stand out from anyone else in those days of frequent population movement, had come to embrace the Lord Almighty as her own God. And she had done so because of the testimony of Naomi's life, however inadequate this may have seemed, and the move of God's Spirit. As was subsequently described in the New Testament regarding a lady named Lydia, she was someone of whom it could be said: *'The Lord opened her heart to respond'* (Acts 16:14). The precise circumstances or timing when Ruth actually turned to God are not known. We can only observe the outward evidence of Ruth's own testimony and that she had *'clung'* to Naomi... all the way back to Bethlehem.

PREOCCUPATION

Because of needing to work through all the bruises and hurts of her own life over those many years, Naomi had not fully realised what God had been doing in the life of Ruth. It can easily be the same for us. We can be so weighed down and preoccupied with pressures and demands that we fail to see the fuller picture of what God has been doing. Sometimes other people, like Naomi's neighbours, unintentionally make things worse by drawing attention to the downside!

The Israelite people were frequently in Naomi's position of having restricted perception. On one occasion God pulled them up by asking a series of pointed questions: *'Why do you say, O Jacob, and complain, O Israel, "My way is hidden from the LORD; my cause is disregarded by my God"? Do you not know? Have you not heard? The LORD is the everlasting God, the Creator of the ends of the earth. He will not grow tired or weary, and his understanding no-one can fathom. He gives strength to the weary and increases the power of the weak'* (Isaiah 40:27–29). Whilst Naomi may have been 'running on empty' and feeling that God had overseen the devastation of her hopes and dreams, together with the loss of identity, God's word through the prophet would soon be made real to her.

GOD'S TIMING

As well as failing to appreciate what God had done in the life of Ruth so that, in fact, Naomi was not actually alone or empty, she had failed to notice something else. The timing of her return to Bethlehem was significant. It was simply recorded at the very end of this first chapter: '... *arriving ... as the barley harvest was beginning.*' This almost throwaway statement was to herald the most important stage of Naomi and Ruth's lives. Yet it is hidden

...He was also working for the future.

away as a seeming after-thought. God had not only been working in the past to bring Ruth to this place through a series of heart-rending calamities, but He was also working for the future. This was unseen to both of these women, but not to God, whose control of timing is as vital as His control over events.

Harvesting grain in Israel at that time took place in April and May. It began with the barley crop and continued with wheat a few weeks later. The narrative in chapter 2 of this book clearly showed that there was a harvest to gather in the first instance. This fact was not to be taken for granted. Not only was there the possibility of the crop failing on account of drought or pestilence, but other factors could also prevent a harvest. Invasion by Israel's enemies and incursions by outside forces to destroy or remove these crops were not unknown events. Gideon, one of the Judge-deliverers raised by God, was recorded as hiding wheat which he was threshing in a winepress (essentially an enclosed space – Judges 6) because of the threat of plunder. As Naomi was returning to Bethlehem at the time of these various Judges, the successful growth and maintenance of these crops was some achievement. God's orchestration of events so that this was a period of relative stability was integral to subsequent events.

GOD IN CONTROL

Whereas many of our circumstances may be within our power to control (to a lesser or greater extent), the time element is something over which we have no jurisdiction... but God does! Time was His idea, setting the sun and stars in place whereby it might be calibrated. Being infinite and eternal in nature, God has no beginning and no ending; Jesus – God who became man – is described as being *'the Alpha and the Omega, the First and the Last, the Beginning and the End'* (Revelation 22:13). He is outside of time and not bound by it. This was why the Jewish religious leaders were incensed by Jesus' comment that *'before Abraham was born, I am'* (John 8:58) because He was pointing to His divinity.

The Bible account highlights the particular work of God in the context of time. Jesus was born *'when the time had fully come'* (Galatians 4:4). He spoke to His mother when at the wedding in Cana of His time having *'not yet come'* (John 2:4), and then in praying to His Father prior to His arrest He declared: *'Father, the time has come. Glorify your Son, that your Son may glorify you'* (John 17:1).

The timing of events that Naomi and Ruth were experiencing was not a coincidence. Arrival in Bethlehem in this period was a harbinger of God about to work in a clear way. Time is in God's hands, as the worship song 'How Great is Our God' (Chris Tomlin) states. Subsequent events affecting these two women was to underline that fact. It is still true for us today. I had been working on some Bible study material and seriously considering contact with a reputable (but secular) publisher with a view to having it self-published. However, just at that time I received an email from a Christian friend about another matter in which he, without knowing of my intentions, volunteered the information that someone he knew (and commended) was setting up his own

Christian self-publication business. I sensed that this was God's intervention and subsequently (and successfully) saw the material emerge in book form from that source.

FOR REFLECTION

1. What factors can affect us so that we end up 'running on empty'?
2. Why can self-preoccupation prevent us from seeing more of what God is doing?
3. In what way can the verses from Isaiah 40:27–31 help us focus on God?
4. Why is it necessary to take timing into account in what is happening in our lives?

7

STEPPING OUT

So she went out and began to glean in the fields
behind the harvesters.
(Ruth 2:3)

READ: RUTH 2:1-3

Decisive moments come to all of us. Some of them loom clearly on the horizon and, perhaps, are forced upon us. An exam to be passed, a career choice to be made, a job application to be submitted, a move to be planned, a relationship to be initiated. Mine was possibly an exception, in terms of the onus lying totally with me – an ending rather than a beginning as I recently took the decision to leave my job after many years' employment. But like all these others, it meant much thought and identification of key factors.

But unfortunately not all such moments are so obvious... or give us time to think. In Ruth's case, the action that she was taking was almost incidental. There was also no question that she would have to step out. It had to be done in order simply to survive. On account of dependence upon an almost totally agricultural economy, working in the fields was the only way ahead for her.

There were various processes that needed to be accomplished in order to harvest a mature crop out in those fields in that period of history. It had, firstly, to be cut with hand sickles and then bound into sheaves. The former was performed by men, the latter by women, who also gathered the stalks of grain that had dropped to the ground and been left behind. The sheaves were then taken to be threshed, which meant that the grain was loosened from the straw. After this process, the grain was tossed into the air with winnowing forks so the remaining straw and chaff was blown away. Finally, the remaining grain was sifted to remove any residual foreign matter.

WELFARE PROVISION

The gathering of those stalks of grain that were left after the crop was cut and bundled into sheaves was termed as 'gleaning'. It was an activity that was especially important in being a form of 'social security' or 'welfare' of that era. Although, perhaps, considered a relatively modern provision in society for helping the poor, destitute or migrant, such 'welfare' or 'benefit' was first instigated many centuries ago. It was decreed by God Himself, being part of the Levitical law for His people. Not only was there to be a supply of income made available to those of the Jewish community, but the law also covered those who came into the territorial boundaries of Israel from outside.

God's provision in this way was laid out as follows: *'When you reap the harvest of your land, do not reap to the very edges of your field or gather the gleanings of your harvest. Leave them for the poor and the alien. I am the LORD your God'* (Leviticus 23:22). Further instructions were recorded in Deuteronomy: *'When you are harvesting in your field and you overlook a sheaf, do not go back to get it. Leave it for the alien, the fatherless and the widow, so that the LORD our God may bless you in all the work of your hands'* (24:19). Foreigners were clearly not ignored by God but included with those who owned no land and therefore had no means of income or livelihood. God explained why He did not miss out this group in the community. *'And you are to love those who are aliens, for you yourselves were aliens in Egypt'* (Deuteronomy 10:19). On this basis the foreigners and poorer members of society were allowed to pick up the leftover pieces of grain and use them in making food.

GETTING PERMISSION

Ruth was therefore able and prepared to take this opportunity to work in the fields as stipulated in the law. However, it's clearly recorded that she first spoke to her mother-in-law. It seemed that she did not assume that Naomi would support her in this action, nor did she assume that she would be allowed to glean in any field even though the law prescribed that she could do so. Perhaps the former was a safeguard for any repercussions arising from the latter. If a landowner was not happy with her, particularly on account of her being a foreigner, then she could always refer to her mother-in-law who was a recognised member of that community. These were uncertain days when *'everyone did as he saw fit'* (Judges 21:25). So Ruth obtained Naomi's permission and blessing as a prudent precaution as well, it may be presumed, as an act of respect and recognition of her standing.

We, as Christians, are also not allowed to act unilaterally, especially when making choices

All decisions... have consequences.

such as those mentioned above. All decisions, especially major ones, have consequences. The input and considerations of other people, particularly those in our spiritual as well as biological families, need to be taken into account. The New Testament writers frequently laid down the need for looking outside of ourselves. The apostle Paul, for instance, wrote: '*Do nothing out of selfish ambition or vain conceit, but in humility consider others better than yourselves. Each of you should look not only to your own interests, but also to the interests of others*' (Philippians 2:3,4).

INTO THE UNKNOWN

However, there was another factor that was important in Ruth's action of stepping out to make a living. She had identified a possible problem when raising this with Naomi; it was by no means certain that she would '*find favour*' (2:2) in the eyes of the owner in whose field she chose to glean. It would seem that there was no way by which she could check on the identity or character of the landowner where she started to work. Google had yet to be invented! Her only course of action was literally to step out in faith, although she may not have specifically viewed it in that light.

Sometimes, even with the technology and sources of information now available, we may be in a similar situation. Like us, Ruth had (as it's sometimes described) to 'suck it and see'. Probably unlike us, however, Ruth had a further complication. In those days the demarcation of property was not very helpful. Fields did not have hedgerows, fences, brick walls or other clear boundaries. Only simple marker stones were placed in the ground to divide the land. It was therefore not necessarily clear as to the extent of the ownership of any field in which Ruth might start to glean.

ANOTHER DAY

So that morning Ruth simply stepped out into a field, and into an amazing destiny... a place where she could '*settle*', finding her

God-gifted identity. Not that it seemed anything like that when she started! That day only held the prospect of back-breaking hard work in the heat of the sun, aiming to get sufficient grain for herself and her mother-in-law to live on. But the day which began with no prospects, only aiming at survival, ended totally differently from her expectations.

God suddenly intervened in a clear way, though He had been working all along. We also should live in faith and hope that God's purposes will be worked out in our lives, even if we cannot see them clearly at the moment, and one day seems to be no different from any other. The outworking of God's promise that *'no good thing does he withhold from those whose walk is blameless'* (Psalm 84:11) may emerge on a day which begins like every other one... but which ends with things radically changed.

THE FIELD

It was through that unknown and uncertain element that God worked – the field in which Ruth was gleaning. The narrative simply states: *'As it turned out, she found herself working in a field belonging to Boaz, who was from the clan of Elimelech'* (2:3). The King James Version uses a quaint turn of phrase: *'... and her hap was to light on a part of the field belonging unto Boaz, who was of the kindred of Elimelech.'* Her action to step out, literally, into that field may have been a completely random movement on Ruth's part...

...God's control over...minor circumstances.

but not to God! The ways in which He works may not always be obvious to us but are always in line with His purposes. Like us, perhaps much of the time, Ruth did not see anything special about what was going on, but events were about to show God's control over even seemingly minor circumstances.

As the account subsequently shows, Boaz wasn't even around when Ruth started to work that morning. So she would not have realised that he was the landowner nor that there was a family connection with him. Neither of them knew each other by sight, and she would not have been able to determine anything of his character. The only precaution that Ruth had apparently taken – a wise one – was to have asked permission of the foreman of the harvesters to start work in that field (see the foreman's reply to Boaz's question, verses 6,7). Apart from that, she had just got on with the task in hand. But that narrative also gives a clue as to the significance of Boaz himself: '... *who was from the clan of Elimelech*'. Elimelech was the name of Ruth's father-in-law... perhaps this throwaway detail was included as if to alert us, the reader, to the fact that things could now be getting particularly interesting!

GOD'S 'COINCIDENCES'

It is said that coincidences are where God choses to act but to remain anonymous. Our understanding of God's ways is too limited to fathom out what He is doing most of the time. But that does not stop us, like Ruth, in getting on with the tasks and responsibilities that lie before us. As the apostle Paul wrote: '*And whatever you do, whether in word or deed, do it all in the name of the Lord Jesus, giving thanks to God the Father through him*' (Colossians 3:17). As we do so, it needs to be with the belief that He works through our circumstances and decisions. There can be that hope (and excitement!) that we are undertaking necessary daily chores through which God breaks through with a 'coincidence'. Some of us may be particularly blessed with having a real vocational call in what we do, and therefore have a sense of fulfilment – if you are in that place, please remember that not all of us can feel the same about where we are.

Whilst there are examples of God breaking through in 'spiritual' surroundings, the Bible clearly records others, like Ruth, who were just getting on with things... then had a God-orchestrated intervention. Gideon, as previously mentioned, was threshing wheat when the angel of the Lord appeared before him, Moses was looking after sheep when he encountered a burning bush – and God. Similarly, the shepherd boy, David, was unexpectedly summoned by Samuel the prophet from looking after the sheep, then anointed as king. Jesus called two of his disciples, Peter and Andrew, when they were hard at work fishing, and then Matthew (in a more sedentary job) when collecting taxes. The Christmas account reminds us of yet more shepherds, this time out in the fields at night guarding their livestock and having an angelic host appear and tell them of the birth of Jesus; that was certainly not in their job description!

...just getting on with things...

So as you read these pages, perhaps on the way to work, during a break in your routine, or before getting into bed after a hard day, remember that God's agenda for you in the next twenty-four hours could involve some significant and obvious move of God in your life, *'As it turned out...'*

FOR REFLECTION

1. How can we involve others in the decisions that we have to make?
2. Why is it important to get on with mundane and routine daily activities?
3. What attitudes can we have to help us pick up the 'coincidences' through which God can be working?
4. How can the realisation that God can intervene in our daily work and routines make a difference to what we do?

8

CONVERSATIONS

At this, she bowed down with her face to the ground.
She exclaimed: 'Why have I found such favour in your eyes
that you notice me – a foreigner?'
(Ruth 2:10)

READ: RUTH 2:4-16

The book of Ruth is remarkable in terms of the amount of conversation that's recorded in its four chapters. Over two thirds of its content contain details of dialogue between the various characters as they interact. Interestingly there is very little information given regarding the physical appearance or age of those involved. The closest that we come to this is in this second chapter, where Boaz, now coming into the picture, described Ruth as a *'young woman'* (2:5). This is in contrast to our present age, where the emphasis is on 'selfies' and 'Facebook' postings, together with fashion sense and being seen using a smart phone. The Bible in general, and this account in Ruth in particular, is more concerned with character and personality. Our words are the means of establishing what we are really like; external looks give very little indication. So the fifty-nine verses in this book describing conversations (out of the overall total of eighty-five) enable us to find out what is actually going on in the hearts and minds of Naomi, Ruth, and now Boaz.

The first words of this man immediately introduce us to someone to whom God is important. He greets his employees, now harvesting the crop, with the words, *'The Lord be with you!'* As previously explained, the word *'Lord'* is the one to describe the Lord God Jehovah (or Yahweh). The response echoes that focus on God: *'"The Lord bless you!" they called back'* (2:4). And then we have a question. If conversation is a prominent feature of this book, then the questions that are posed are even more revealing. The opening chapter alone has six of them, all but one being asked by Naomi, and each of hers exposing the depths of her care, anxiety and confusion... but also showing that somehow she was wanting to make sense of what was happening. Now we have Boaz who follows up his God-centred declaration with a question. And it's not one that we might expect: *'Whose young woman is that?'* (2:5).

BEING NOTICED

Boaz's probing of his foreman who's been overseeing the harvesting of his crop immediately shows some further important aspects of his character. Firstly, he makes space and time to look around. If he had not done so, then he would not have noticed Ruth. Bearing in mind the time of the year when this question was asked it is not to be glossed over. Boaz was a very busy man, a landowner overseeing an agricultural business on which his livelihood, and that of his community, depended. It was a season of the year when everything was coming to a head – all systems go! A harvest to be reaped, productivity to be maximised, waste and overheads to be reduced to a minimum, and close attention to costs, not to mention the weather. But here was Boaz, one eye on his iPad for updates, his mind whirling with figures... and he still notices someone whom he's not seen before. This girl – probably amongst a crowd of others,

> ... he still notices someone... unknown and anonymous.

the strugglers and no-hopers of society, with no prospects and no status – was noticed even though unknown and anonymous.

As this account progresses, we shall see that Boaz is a type (or 'shadow') of Jesus. There are strong traits in his character that point to the love and care of the Son of God. The fact that Boaz noticed Ruth is reflective of the occasions when Jesus also noticed people to whom others were oblivious. The widow placing two small coins into the temple treasury, the woman suffering from bleeding who simply touched His clothes, the helpless paralysed man amongst the crowds of disabled by the pool of Bethesda, and the Samaritan woman whom He met at the well, ostracised by everyone else. These and others were noticed by Jesus... whose eyes still notice people like you and me, those on the fringes, hidden in the crowd, sitting at the back, quiet among all the voices calling for attention. This was Ruth; this is us, perhaps quite a lot of the time.

A CARING HEART

Secondly, Boaz's question was not only indicative of an observant eye but also of a caring heart. He would not have given Ruth the 'time of day', let alone bother to make an enquiry about her, if there had not been some deeper motive than simply wanting factual information. There are occasions in the Bible where God Himself is recorded as asking questions. Clearly the reason for doing so is not because of any ignorance on the part of the

All-knowing, All-wise and All-mighty God! We have to look for another purpose behind the questions that God poses. The fact is that He already knows the answer... but do we? Rather like a sympathetic and good schoolteacher, He puts questions in order for the student to realise something of which they had not previously been aware.

For that reason we find that Jesus asked questions during the course of His ministry. *'How many loaves do you have?' 'Where have you laid him?' 'Do you want to get well?' 'Why do you call me good?' 'Who touched Me?' 'Where is your faith?'* (Mark 8:5; John 11:34; John 5:6; Mark 10:18; Mark 5:31; Luke 8:25). Behind all of these questions – even beyond the need for the hearer to see deeper motives or understanding – was the heart of God displaying His care and love, though the latter may have been of the 'tough' variety. The care which Boaz displayed towards Ruth even in that simple enquiry was soon to be shown as the harbinger of something more, apparent in his subsequent direct conversation with her and then in action that he instigated.

> ...the harbinger of something more...

PRACTICAL CONCERN

The enquiry that Boaz made to his foreman also brought out a third aspect of his character, that of his concern in practical ways. As previously mentioned, women in general, and foreigners in particular, were not viewed as having any status in society. Although Jewish culture underlined their value as people (as distinct from being mere chattels), those days were, nevertheless, extremely patriarchal in outlook. The Levitical law enabled women to have certain rights, but equality of sexes was not even on the distant horizon. However, Boaz was not only aware of

58

the legal obligation that he needed to fulfil towards the poor, widowed and foreigner, but rigorously enforced it. He made sure that those in whose hands he placed responsibility for the day-to-day running of his business carried out those provisions. The foreman's answer to his employer showed this to be the case: *'The foreman replied, "She is the Moabitess who came back from Moab with Naomi. She said, 'Please let me glean and gather among the sheaves behind the harvesters.' She went into the field and has worked steadily from morning till now"'* (2:7). Ruth had been allowed to carry out the gleaning of the crops in that particular field in accordance with God's direction through Moses.

This practical concern of Boaz was clearly an integral part of his life, the outworking of his close relationship with God. It was not something that came and went when it was convenient, or when needing to make some kind of impression. The New Testament writers inevitably included instructions to the groups of Christians under their care that their lifestyle was to involve showing godly love and practical kindness to everyone, all the time. Especially is this needed when, like Boaz coming to his field and noticing Ruth, circumstances arise which are unexpected.

A MURKY BACKGROUND?

Lastly, the question that Boaz asked his foreman displayed an empathy and sympathy for someone who, as a foreigner coming into the land of Israel at this time of instability, was most likely to have been bruised and battered by events and circumstances. She was therefore likely to be particularly vulnerable and struggling with her sense of identity.

Perhaps that was because Boaz himself had experienced the emotional trials of life. Many years later, the Gospel writer

Matthew set out the human genealogy of Jesus, tracing this back to Abraham. However, as he listed the relevant names the one for Boaz was followed by the words '... *whose mother was Rahab*' (Matthew 1:5). This was the same Canaanite, pagan-orientated resident of Jericho, back in the time of Joshua, who was also described as a *'prostitute'* (Joshua 2:1). Although that city had been totally destroyed, she and her family were spared. This was on account of her hiding the Israelite spies from the authorities and enabling them to escape, driven by a fear of the Lord God. Rahab had subsequently married an Israelite named Salmon. It might be conjectured that he was actually one of those two spies! But however that marriage came about, it is possible that there could have been underlying prejudices, gossip and ostracism arising from that union and the little family that emerged. This murky background would have made Boaz alert to the kind of feelings that Ruth was experiencing, and the need for support.

God, too, is not unaware of the kind of circumstances that surround our lives in terms of stigma. Indeed, His own Son was born to an unmarried girl into a working class family and community ruled by a harsh government of an invading power. His empathy towards us is described as follows: '*For we do not have a high priest who is unable to sympathise with our weaknesses, but we have one who has been tempted in every way, just as we are – yet was without sin. Let us then approach the throne of grace with confidence, so that we may receive mercy and find grace to help us in our time of need*' (Hebrews 4:15,16).

A CRUCIAL CONVERSATION

With these underlying perspectives regarding Boaz's question, and the foreman's reply, identifying Ruth as this unknown young woman who had been noticed, the account immediately records the next conversation. This is the crucial initial one between Boaz and Ruth herself. It seems that the former wasted no time in going to speak to her. Whilst he may have had scheduled appointments, deadlines to meet and plans to make, he still made time to speak to this otherwise unknown stranger.

Boaz's kind response to Ruth's plight, reassuring her of protection and provision as long as she's careful to glean within his fields meets with an immediate reply. It's another question! *'Why have I found such favour in your eyes that you notice me – a foreigner?'* (2:10) These totally unexpected words of affirmation from him literally cause her to bow down with her face to the ground (in surprise as well as respect, maybe?). She's immediately registered the fact that she's been noticed, but that her status did not qualify her for this to happen. In her mind she did not even have the standing of one of his servant girls. Boaz's reply revealed a different perspective on her situation. She was looking at her ranking in society, but he was viewing her as someone who'd taken an enormous step into the unknown – a leap of faith – arising from commitment to the Lord God. Using beautiful imagery, Boaz described her as being under God's *'wings'* where she had *'come to take refuge'* (2:12). He had prefaced this by describing the emotional and physical ties from which she had chosen to break away in order to take this step.

WORDS BRING LIFE

Ruth was clearly more appreciative of Boaz's kind and affirming words than, perhaps, anything else. In physical terms nothing had changed. She remained a destitute alien on the edge of society with no prospects or hope of change. But those words from Boaz touched her inner being, that part of her which had, no doubt, been hardened against comfort ever been spoken to her again, on account of the hurt and devastation she had previously experienced. They were also words that started to bring that needed sense of significance and specialness. She said to Boaz: *'You have given me comfort and have spoken kindly to your servant...'* (2:13). They may have been only words, but they had power to penetrate and bring a change of perspective. Words from God are life-restoring and life-changing. Jesus emphasised this: *'The words I have spoken to you are spirit and they are life'* (John 6:63).

Boaz's words were a foretaste of what was to happen in practical terms. This was described as follows: *'At mealtime Boaz said to her, "Come over here. Have some bread and dip it in the wine vinegar." When she sat down with the harvesters, he offered her some roasted grain. She ate all she wanted and had some left over'* (2:14). But it was words that first touched Ruth... as they can touch us. God may bring questions that need to alert us to issues that we need to address, but also He is still able to speak, *'kindly'*, into our lost hopes and identities, to bring comfort and life.

FOR REFLECTION

1. Why is it important that we have the sense of being noticed by other people (in a positive way)... and by God?

2. What does Psalm 139 tell us about God's awareness of us?

3. What do you think was significant about the phrase used by Boaz, *'under whose wings you have come to take refuge'* (2:12)?

4. How might the words and actions of Boaz have contributed to Ruth's sense of worth and identity at this time?

9

CONNECTIONS

He has not stopped showing his kindness to the living and the dead.
(Ruth 2:20)

READ: RUTH 2:19–23

Sophisticated technology to which we have ready access now enables us to keep in touch with people and events around the globe, seemingly all the time. But this is not entirely good news. An article in a London newspaper looked at this aspect under the heading: 'How to survive the email overload[3]'. It stated that seven out of ten workers living in the city and south-east of the country admitted to feeling stress on account of the volume of information bombarding them each day. One in three revealed that this was affecting their mental health and family relationships. An example was given of a professional who, in one day, received 271 work-related emails and over 100 text messages. But only a fraction of these were personally directed to her and needed an immediate

---

3   Evening Standard (London, England) 5.11.15

response. The key to handling all of these communications was, somehow, to sift and identify these specifically targeted ones. 'Digital detox' – severing all ties with cyberspace – is apparently being taken by an increasing number of people as the ultimate solution!

But whilst many of us are spared such high volumes of communications in the many and varied ways in which they come to us, sifting and assessing still remain important tasks in our lives. Determining those events and situations which need our attention either straightaway or in due course is an on-going activity.

QUICK QUESTIONS

So as this account in respect of Ruth continues, we come to a point where a vital assessment has to be made. When Ruth had returned at the end of the day after gleaning the leftovers from crops which had been cut down in the field, her mother-in-law was anxious to find out what had been happening... and to sift through the information that was disclosed. In fact, Naomi hadn't even waited to hear what Ruth had to say. She had immediately noticed what Ruth had brought back home: *'So Ruth gleaned in the field until evening. Then she threshed the barley she had gathered, and it amounted to about an ephah. She carried it back to town, and her mother-in-law saw how much she had gathered. Ruth also brought out and gave her what she had left over after she had eaten enough'* (2:17,18). The quantity of provision from that day's activity spoke volumes!

Naomi's quick-fire questions to Ruth, *'Where did you glean today? Where did you work?'* didn't even allow space for an answer to be given. They were immediately followed up with a statement: *'Blessed be the man who took notice of you!'* (2:19). Whatever else was going on in Naomi's life at that time, and whatever pressures she was needing to handle, everything now stopped. Ruth's situation, probably high on the agenda anyway, now became the number one priority. Rather like stumbling across an email in a crowded inbox that suddenly attracts our attention, or an out-of-the-blue phone call picked up in a hectic schedule, everything else was now pushed to one side.

Although Ruth had, by some means not disclosed in the narrative, learnt of the identity of the owner of the field in which she had been working and who had shown her considerable kindness, this was not significant to her. So when she told Naomi that his name was Boaz, it may have been said in a very matter-of-fact tone. Whatever his actions and attitude, which were actually quite remarkable, at the end of the day Ruth had remained a widowed poor foreigner who was in 'survival mode'. Irrespective of his identity, her outward circumstances and prospects had not changed.

CHANGED!

However, to Naomi, everything had changed! Her immediate reaction to this simple piece of information, added to the tangible evidence of his godliness, was to exclaim, 'The LORD bless him!' (2:20). Whether or not at this point Naomi was leaping around with joy and hugging her daughter-in-law is not recorded. She was certainly taking this news as something that was significant... and a reason to praise God. Because now, after long years of harsh circumstances and hopelessness, not only had God's care been shown in a general way by reason of Him providing food for His people, which had meant that Naomi had been able to return home, but Ruth had almost literally stumbled into a situation

...Ruth had ... stumbled into a situation...

which pointed to God's specific care. As Naomi explained: *'That man is our close relative; he is one of our kinsman-redeemers'* (2:20). A connection had suddenly been made which was to open up a significant development in both of their lives.

This term that Naomi used, 'kinsman-redeemer', pointed to the status that Boaz held. The Levitical law, given by Moses and inspired by God, placed great emphasis on stewardship of the land. In a mainly agricultural society the land was not only important for growing crops and generating an income, but in sustaining life and enabling succeeding generations of God's people to grow up. For this reason, the Promised Land was not only divided into specific territorial areas between each of the tribes of Israel, but within those territories it was parcelled out between the different family groupings. The book of Joshua allocates nine chapters (13 to 21) to describing territories that still needed to be subdued, or were earmarked to the many groups within each tribe. The place names and geographical locations may be tongue-twisters to us, and hold no meaning, but it showed the principal role that land held.

KINSMAN-REDEEMER

As we have also noted, such an economy could be dramatically affected by climatic and political factors, not to mention poor farming techniques and divine affliction. So the law that Moses was inspired to draw up took into account the possible loss of land which a family might suffer. It might need to be sold off to pay debts or raise capital; people might need to sell themselves off for this purpose. The Year of Jubilee was set aside as the time when land was to be restored to its original owners, and for those in slavery to be released. It was a designated twelve-month period that was to take place every forty-nine or fifty years (there is some ambiguity as to precisely how many). But in the meantime there was provision for a close relative (kinsman- redeemer) to step in and buy back land (or people) into family ownership which had been sold off (perhaps we would use the term 'leased'). This action was described as 'redeeming' the land (see Leviticus 25:21–28, 47–49). Over a period of time this was linked to a further law whereby if an Israelite died without an heir then his brother was obliged to marry the childless widow in order to ensure continuation of the family line (Deuteronomy 25:5).

Because it is almost certain that the practice of this Year of Jubilee was never actually carried out by the Children of Israel, certainly not in a widespread way, this process of redemption was the only means to retrieve land (and people) that had been, or was likely to be, sold off. In Naomi and Ruth's case, it was apparent that the former's husband, Elimelech, had owned a family plot prior to having to leave for Moab and find provision of food. This land had remained uncultivated since that time and no male member of the family was now alive to farm it. The future for Naomi in respect of ownership (needing to sell in order to raise funds) and of the family line now looked bleak.

The appearance of Boaz onto the scene, and Naomi's realisation of his position as one of these kinsman-redeemers prompted her to instruct Ruth regarding her immediate future. She was to remain with his workers, something that she had already been told by Boaz himself. Naomi underlined the importance of this action, a reminder of the volatility and instability of those times in which they were living: '... *because in someone else's field you might be harmed*' (2:22). The last verse of this chapter confirmed that Ruth fully complied with what her mother-in-law had directed. '*So Ruth stayed close to the servant girls of Boaz to glean until the barley and wheat harvests were finished*' (2:23).

ENCOURAGEMENT AND SUPPORT

What may at first sight have seemed a random or coincidental step by Ruth in going into that field owned by Boaz was now emerging as the link by which a particular connection was made. This was to prove pivotal. God is still in the business of bringing about such 'connections' through which people are to be influential in our lives. This is, no doubt, the experience of many Christians in finding (as was to be the case with Ruth) their future spouse. But other vital and God-honouring friendships can also result from seemingly unplanned meetings. The apostle

...seemingly unplanned meetings...

Paul frequently described people being brought into his life through whom he received godly encouragement and support in his ministry. It is probably the case that none of these were previous 'Facebook friends' whom he had known when a fanatical Christian-hating Pharisee! All of them were brought about by God in many and diverse ways. The brief references to those whom Paul greeted when writing his letter to the church in Rome (chapter 16) provides an example of such 'connections'.

Two longstanding friendships show something of the way in which God worked in my own life through 'connections'. One of my spiritual mentors was someone whom I first met when we were both involved in church youth work in different parts of London. Initially coming into contact through a sports event which we both 'happened' to help organise, we continued to keep in touch well after our age rendered such youth club work inappropriate! But now our similar outlook and commitment to God deepened our sharing and support, which has been the basis of continuing friendship. These spiritual ties also developed with another friend whom I'd first known when studying in the sixth form. A gap of many years followed before he 'happened' to be invited to a church service where I was giving the talk. I hadn't recognised him, but when he came up to introduce himself afterwards I realised who he was and we immediately 'clicked'.

God's intention for Ruth was not only for her to be in a particular geographical location and set of circumstances, but also to be connected to specific people. It was through these that He was working to achieve His purposes for her life and highlight her identity. Naomi was clearly one of these people. Boaz was also now to be someone very significant in Ruth's life in enabling her to find a place to 'settle'.

FOR REFLECTION

1. In what positive ways can people with whom we initially 'connect' influence and help us?

2. In what areas of life are we most likely to meet with people with whom we 'connect' as a starting point to friendship?

3. What part do you feel that God now plays in bringing people alongside us as those with whom we 'connect'?

4. What personal qualities do you consider enable you to make good and positive 'connections' with other people?

10

FINDING
A HOME

My daughter, should I not try to find a home for you,
where you will be well provided for?
(Ruth 3:1)

READ: RUTH 3:1,2

The advertisement was blunt. It was also one that could not be missed. Being inches from my face as I stood in a crowded rush-hour Tube train the heading for the advert was simple: 'No one should have no one at Christmas.'[4] Under that headline it continued to advocate that no one should be without somebody else with whom to share Christmas lunch, pull a cracker or open a present. It aimed at raising the profile of older people likely to be alone during the festive period. However, the strong image that it presented could equally apply to the rest of the year and to a sizable swathe of the population alongside pensioners; people who, for the most part, live in isolation, not just at Christmas.

Statistics point to a disturbing fact. An increasing number of

---

4   ageuk.org.uk

people in the UK are living alone. Figures released by the Office of National Statistics showed that 29 per cent of households in 2013 were occupied by only one person[5]. This represented 7.7 million people, half a million more than ten years previously, and a massive 1 million increase since 2001. The percentage figure for London was even greater – 35 per cent of households had single occupiers in 2011. The pressure to build new housing is just one evidence of this increase in those living much of their time alone.

A RHETORICAL QUESTION

People in that situation, whether by default or design, is not new. Whilst Ruth in the Old Testament lived with Naomi, her mother-on-law, and was therefore not actually alone, her single status was identified as not being the best situation for her. So the question directed at her was more rhetorical than inquisitorial: '... *should I not try to find a home for you...?*' (3:1; '... *shall I not seek rest for thee...?*', KJV). The Hebrew word from which '*home*' and '*rest*' are derived can also mean 'place of rest', 'state of rest' and 'security'. There would have been social expectations, economic pressures, physiological issues and practical aspects that constituted the 'mix' behind this question. But they were not the main reasons behind this mother-in-law's statement.

COMMUNITY

Behind Naomi's words was, along with other vital factors, the realisation that well-being and development of character, identity and gifting do not take place only when alone. Whilst there is a need for 'space' and reflecting whilst away from others, there is much that can only be achieved through relationships.

---

5   www.ons.gov.uk/ons/rel/family-demography/familes-and-households/2013/stb-families-html'

Such relationships are God's gift to enable us to become the people that He wants us to be – and to develop our sense of identity. Long before sociologists conducted their studies to confirm the benefits of 'community', the psalmist was inspired to write: '*A father to the fatherless, a defender of widows, is God in his holy dwelling. God sets the lonely in families, he leads forth the prisoners with singing...*' (Psalm 68:5,6). There is more than a physiological downside to isolation, though this is clearly bad enough and typified by a national newspaper columnist's article, headed 'Marriage works, and it's the answer to the misery of loneliness'. In it he pointed out that there was a significant increase in the prescription of antidepressants to those living alone as distinct from those who had a partner.[6]

Throughout the Bible, both community and relationships form the foundation on which God – who Himself is a mysterious yet perfect community of Father, Son and Holy Spirit – is carrying out His purposes on this earth. In the Old Testament it was particularly through the tribal groupings of the Children of Israel. The New Testament saw the formation of local fellowships of believers that made up the Church through which God worked.

Naomi was very much aware of 'community' in terms of the tribes, clans and families of the Old Testament. It was noticeable that when she chose to return to her homeland following the end of the famine that she went back to Bethlehem. This was the place where she and her husband had previously lived and been part of the community. In theory she might have gone anywhere in Israel. But her roots lay in that town, together with the property that

...her roots lay in that town...

had now become her own, following the death of her husband and the absence of any male heir. This ownership of land was one of the 'drivers' instigated by God to facilitate keeping people together in 'community', as well as being essential in maintaining physical life.

EMPLOYMENT AND SPORT

Fast-forward to the twenty-first century and it's noticeable that many people find their place of work as their focal point in terms of 'community' and relationships. This is partly on practical grounds. The long periods of time needing to be spent at work in order to earn sufficient wages is one of these, together with the ethos which many employees are required to 'buy into' as part of their employment. Even those who don't see their work as a 'career' with all its demands and expectations are now subjected to pressure from management in various ways. These include participation in 'bonding' exercises, 'teamwork' meetings and operating as part of a 'group'.

Having worked in an office environment for a long time, it's been very obvious to me that colleagues have also found the workplace to be the main (if not only) source of their social lives and, for some, the springboard to finding a spouse or partner. Employment can therefore be the means by which many people find their sense of worth, purpose and identity.

But there is a downside. This particularly arises when circumstances change with regard to work. Even disregarding the considerable socialising aspect, the loss of a job through redundancy, fixed-term contracts, sacking or retirement can be devastating. This is not only because of a loss or reduction of income, but also in removing the sense of worth, status and ability to contribute. However, even within the work environment there can be situations that arise which bring a similar effect. Whilst I was working within a specialist team in a government department, we were suddenly the subject of management reorganisation. The result of this was that our work, in which we had built up a considerable amount of expertise and effectiveness with the public and other networks over many years, was removed within a very short period of time. There was no provision for negotiation, no advice sought from us regarding possible repercussions, and no regard paid to what we had achieved. My colleagues and I, with these many accumulated years of recognised skills, were powerless and now having to look for other roles within the organization. It felt as though we were simply pawns subjected to the undisclosed agendas of other people. This did not positively contribute to our collective or individual sense of identity!

The area of sport is another one from which many people derive a sense of identity. Media coverage seems to promote this aspect, whatever the shape or size of the ball that the sport involves. But a serious downside can apply, as with employment. This is especially if the team that's followed is one which struggles and languishes in the lower leagues of their profession (as is the case with Leyton Orient, my local professional soccer side!).

NAOMI'S PERCEPTION

Ruth may not have been subjected to management machinations which caused her to feel powerless and anonymous. She certainly had no career lined up for her in Bethlehem arising from some LinkedIn headhunting internet connection! But neither, unlike her mother-in-law, did she have any roots or property in the town which acted as a means of connection. There were certainly no cultural ties with which to link when arriving in Israel. Quite the opposite, since her upbringing and adult lifestyle within the boundaries of Moab and its spiritual atmosphere would have made Naomi's country feel very alien to her. The means by which she could find her sense of God-gifted identity through being part of that community were almost non-existent.

However, Naomi had seen Ruth find herself work in a safe environment of a more-than-benevolent landowner, and labour alongside others perhaps in a similar position to herself. Naomi was providing Ruth with support and company as together they were able to find food. But, no doubt aware of all these other factors, Naomi perceived that there was something more needed for her daughter-in-law.

> ...clearly identified with God's people.

Essentially, Naomi believed that Ruth needed a significant relationship – to be married. By this means, if for no other reason, there would be the opportunity to integrate into that community to which she was, as yet, an outsider. She would thereby experience being valued and supported as someone who was not only a believer in God, as Ruth had indeed become, but one who clearly identified with God's people. This was something which Ruth herself had wanted when declaring to Naomi back in Moab, *'Your people shall be my people, and your God my God'* (1:16). The importance of the former may not have been fully recognised by her as being necessary to understanding her God-gifted identity. But now her mother-in-law was setting in motion the means by which it could be outwardly evidenced as well as being a spiritual fact.

THE CHURCH

This is where the Church, prefigured by those Old Testament tribal and community ties which God had put in place, has a particular relevance. It is now through the *'family of believers'* (Galatians 6:10; *'household of faith'*, KJV) that a supportive environment of acceptance and value can be experienced. Whilst the term 'Church' may currently present many connotations – not all of them very positive – the original Greek word actually meant 'assembly' or 'congregation'. This was in the particular context of people as distinct from a type of architecture, an organisation or institution. And this is not just 'people' as with those being part of a 'club' or 'workforce'. Having a relationship with God as our *Father* and seeing one another as *brothers* and *sisters* shows the Church as being God's family. The Church is also compared to being a bride, in whom God delights and cares, a *body* in which everyone has a vital part to play, and a *building* whom God joins together for a purpose (see Ephesians 5:21–33; 1 Corinthians 12:12–31; Ephesians 2:20–22; 1 Peter 2:4,5; James 2:15; 1 John 2:15, 3:1, 3:17).

The New Testament not only describes local churches as organising Sunday services. There was a great deal more! *'They devoted themselves to the apostles' teaching and to the fellowship, to the breaking of bread and to prayer. Everyone was filled with awe, and wonders and miraculous signs were done by the apostles. All the believers were together and had everything in common. Selling their possessions and goods, they gave to anyone as he had need. Every day they continued to meet together in the temple courts. They broke bread in their homes and ate together with glad and sincere hearts, praising God and enjoying the favour of all the people. And the Lord added to their number daily those who were being saved'* (Acts 2:42–47). The flavour of what God was doing in and through a group of local Christians is clearly evident. People were not only being enabled to find God and experience His life-changing power, but in so doing were coming to realise their identity in God.

The following chapters in Acts, along with the letters to other churches outside Jerusalem, showed people now being enabled to move on in their journey with God and His purposes for their lives. This is why it's still vital for every believer to be part of a (preferably) local church family. As with a biological one, it provides for nurturing, supporting, maturing, giving and enlarging which contribute to growth as a Christian. It was through such a spiritual community that Ruth was to find more of her own identity, a place to *settle*.

FOR REFLECTION

1. What other factors may have contributed to Ruth feeling that she was an outsider when arriving in Bethlehem with Naomi?
2. In what ways do you feel that Naomi and Boaz (in the initial stage) had been able to help Ruth start to become part of the community where she now lived?
3. From what other sources, as well as work and employment, do people now draw a sense of worth and value?
4. What positive experiences have you had in being connected with a local church?
5. How can people be helped to move from the 'fringe' into a greater sense of 'belonging' to a local church?

11

BELONGING

One day Naomi her mother-in-law said to her, 'My daughter, should I not try to find a home for you, where you will be well provided for?'
(Ruth 3:1)

READ: RUTH 3:1,2

The packet was carefully unsealed and the instruction sheet located. The enclosed medication was one of several prescriptions that my brother had collected following hospital discharge. Each of them had specified dosages and daily intake frequencies. But first of all there were those instructions. When unfolded it revealed a large volume of details in small print... and it was not good news! Copious warnings, precautions, ominous side-effects and emergency procedures were spelt out. Reading these raised the question as to whether actually taking the capsules was the best course of action at all! Those health alerts seem to far outweigh the benefits.

Of course, such health warnings are not limited to the field of medicine. They seem to arise in almost every activity that we now undertake. Packaged food always includes postings of this nature, and public transport is another area where warning signs occur at every point. These cautions, wherever their location, underline the risks and uncertainties that now exist.

But health warnings also apply in connection with our journey of faith. God wants us to trust Him because *'We live by faith, not by sight'* (2 Corinthians 5:7). And that can be scary! It's especially unnerving when God gives us a 'nudge' that we need to move on.

A RISKY STEP

That's what Naomi's question to Ruth, her daughter-in-law, was indicating... the need for change, together with an implicit health warning. She not only had in mind the means by which marriage would enable Ruth to be integrated into the community, and the beneficial effects in a general way. Naomi also phrased her question to indicate the specific effects of having a 'home' and being, 'well provided for'. These were not only going to make a tangible difference to Ruth's outward circumstances. They were also going to bring her a specific sense of belonging and acceptance, and remove the feeling of vulnerability. Each of these was an element in building an awareness of her identity.

But in Ruth's case, marriage was not an automatic and easy course of action. Which made Naomi's belief in it even more important. There were huge factors to take into account when considering this step, about which she would have been fully aware. These included Ruth being a foreigner with a staunchly anti-God background. Marriage by the Israelites to those who had previously occupied the Promised Land was strictly forbidden and therefore, by inference, only allowed with fellow Israelites. Many years later, God spoke through the reforms of Nehemiah to broaden this restriction. The men of Judah were reprimanded for marrying women from outside nations, including Moab (Ruth's country of origin), this being described as having led the nation into sin (Nehemiah 13:23–27).

Additionally, Ruth was someone with no social standing, no prospects and no children. Overall, her CV was distinctly unimpressive! But despite these considerable drawbacks and associated risks, Naomi still held a proactive stance with regard to changing Ruth's situation. She saw marriage as being more than meeting cultural expectations and being expedient.

NEEDING CHANGE

What follows needs a health alert! Naomi indicated in that statement to Ruth, specifically wanting her to find that place of rest and security, that she was not currently in such a state. She needed a significant relationship which would have repercussions in terms of her practical, emotional and spiritual well-being... having that sense of her God-gifted identity. Fast-forward three millennia, and we come to a delicate area of life needing care and openness, whether being looked at personally or within the context of a church family. Ruth's situation, as Naomi viewed it at that point, could equally be applied to ourselves in similarly spiritually dark times. The problem is that, unlike Ruth's experience with her mother-in-law, this is not necessarily acknowledged or adequately addressed.

SINGLENESS – A PRACTICAL ISSUE

Three aspects of Ruth's situation are relevant to ourselves. The first of these was that Naomi identified relationship, particularly in the context of singleness, as a very practical issue. She was prepared to face up to it and take specific action. This meant initially shouldering responsibility and raising it with Ruth. But, as we shall see, the latter was not going to be allowed to sit back and wait for things to happen. Naomi's attitude was not of seeing singleness as a permanent state. Neither did she see it as automatically changing, something into which she would effortlessly slip. Further, she highlighted moving into close relationship and marriage as essential for Ruth's particular well-being, even in respect of someone who had now come to have a relationship with God and wanting to be part of a community of God's people.

> ...essential for Ruth's ... well-being...

Singleness remains a very practical aspect of our lives as Christians, whatever our current status, and the churches which constitute our spiritual homes. And there are large numbers who are in that place of singleness whether separated, divorced, bereaved or never married. According to the book *No Sex Please, We're Single*, written by Ian Gregory (Kingsway, 2002), 35 per cent of adults in UK evangelical churches are single, with the trend being an upward one, reflecting the increasing number of people generally who are living alone. So although the majority of those in churches are, potentially, supported by a spouse, there remain a big proportion of Christians who are essentially on their own.

A SNAPSHOT

So what acknowledgement is there in respect of those who are single which is equivalent to that shown by Naomi for Ruth? It's generally acknowledged that contemporary marriages are under considerable stress. In the UK there are many support mechanisms in place for Christians who are married. There are courses for marriage preparation, marriage enrichment, marriage and parenting, and marriage break-up recovery, to name but a few. Google the words 'church marriage courses' and there would be over 100 million results. However, a search for 'church singleness courses' would show only a fraction of that figure (0.5 million), with none of them actually indicating any 'course' or similar provision. Bible Week events perhaps back up this snapshot. Amongst all the scheduled workshops there would be, typically, just one with a focus on singleness, compared to a larger number dealing with marriage-related issues.

A similar picture is presented in many church programmes consisting simply of Sunday services, weekday home groups and opportunities for helping run various activities. But what about the rest of the time? In practical terms there seems to be little recognition that, for example, many single Christians come home to an empty house or flat after a stressful day at work in a (probably) secular environment, with no one to provide ready support, encouragement and opportunity to share with. And this is a scenario that's repeated day after day. Naomi identified Ruth's current situation as not being the best. She inferred that it did not constitute a spiritually healthy situation. The question that was consequently raised with Ruth might still be relevant today.

PRAY!

The practical nature of singleness meant more than acknowledgement. Naomi's statement to Ruth indicated positive action. The demands and limited resources of today's local churches probably restrict the opportunity for ongoing support. The use of social media and internet sites in this whole area of singleness has attendant risks and shortfalls.

But at least we can pray! The biblical examples of Isaac praying for Rebekah, Hannah praying for herself, and Zechariah and Elizabeth for themselves, all in respect of wanting children when in situations of barrenness and hopelessness are particularly encouraging. Theirs was also an aspect of life with which they were struggling largely alone. But they also viewed the situation as something which they could bring to God and experience change.

Many churches now incorporate specific time during a Sunday service where people can receive individual prayer for specific issues. The sensitive nature of sickness, debt, addiction, unemployment, homelessness and childlessness can all be brought to God in prayer. Singleness, the need for close friendship and perhaps wanting to be married can be specified amongst these others as areas in which ongoing prayer support can be provided in the context of the church family. As Paul wrote: *'Carry each other's burdens, and in this way you will fulfil the law of Christ'* (Galatians 6:2).

At the very least it's noticeable that Naomi was alert to Ruth's situation. This is not to be taken for granted. Perhaps the need for such awareness regarding singleness was typified in a sermon on adultery, and the broader aspect of sexually improper activity which I heard. It was rightly pointed out that the principle way of avoidance was to have a strong marital relationship. What was omitted, however, was any suggestion or mention as how a single person was to cope with pressures associated with that commandment. For someone like that, there was no spouse around... and in this instance, such a scenario wasn't acknowledged. (To be fair, when discussed with the speaker after the service this omission was subsequently remedied.)

SINGLENESS – AN EMOTIONAL ISSUE

Secondly, the reason for Naomi's proactive stance in respect of Ruth was not only at a practical level, but also emotional. She could identify with her daughter-in-law in terms of having lived in an alien culture, grieving the loss of a husband, and trying to live out a life of godliness in a spiritually dark environment. She recognised that emotional stability and security was part of a good and godly marriage which singleness would not readily provide. Hence her specific reference to Ruth having a place of 'rest' (3:1, word used in King James version for 'home')''.

The book *No Sex Please, We're Single* pointed out that singleness had a significant pastoral impact in today's churches. This might not be directly attributed to that status, but the underlying cause could be a lack of meaningful relationship that God intended to be primarily met by means of a marriage partner; close friendships also being of value. Those weekly Sunday service and home group meeting are, in reality, starvation-diet levels of relationship input

> ...starvation-diet levels of relationship input...

for a single person. This is particularly relevant when singles are having to contend with a pressured secular work regime, the pace of life, possible family responsibilities and lack of hope that anything will change. Loneliness, lack of self-worth and self-confidence, depression, addictions and workaholism are possible fallouts. These have to be acknowledged as well as put alongside other aspects of singleness. The latter include possibly having more time and energy to serve God in specific ways, availability to provide company for others, and having greater flexibility.

Even the secular world appreciates that loneliness is a serious problem. Age Concern UK report that 1 million older people will have had no meaningful contact with another person in over a month. Naomi was not unaware of this situation when she talked to Ruth... neither is God, who inspired the writer of Ecclesiastes: *'If one falls down, his friend can help him up. But pity the man who falls and has no-one to help him up! Also, if two lie down together, they will keep warm. But how can one keep warm alone? Though one may be overpowered, two can defend themselves'* (4:10–12). Marriage in particular can enable husband and wife to act as a godly 'mirror' to each other to bring affirmation and Christ-like character.

Perhaps a question might be asked of those who are single within church fellowships along the following lines: How many times a week are you aware that you are alone and single, and want that to be different in some way? The response might be quite revealing in terms of the pressure that it indicates. Did Naomi ever ask that question of Ruth? Perhaps she didn't need to... she knew the answer.

A SPIRITUAL ISSUE

Whilst Naomi was very down to earth in her approach to Ruth, she was also someone who was spiritually sensitive. She thirdly identified marriage as providing a spiritual element in their environment of general godlessness and self-centeredness. The narrative describes how this worked out, as we shall see. At this point her sensitivity was shown by her focus on Boaz, the landowner in whose field Ruth had been working. This was not only because of those family ties that existed and resolving the important issue of land ownership. It was also because of his spirituality by which he had already begun to build up Ruth's sense of significance and specialness – her identity – in the form of the kind words that he had spoken and action that he'd taken.

Relationship in general, and marriage in particular, is shown in the Bible as being God's idea, His plan and a prophetic picture. The account of Ruth showed God working in the life of an unlikely person to be part of Jesus' human genealogy. But it also demonstrated Him bringing people into relationship with Himself and into God-honouring close relationship with each other. Ruth is a beautiful example of these spiritual aspects, arising from the attitude and actions of Naomi. It was this mother-in-law who succinctly highlighted the importance of significant relationship for Ruth, a means to strengthen and grow her sense of identity.

FOR REFLECTION

1. Why do you think that Naomi was upfront about Ruth needing to be married?
2. What do you feel was Ruth's possible response to Naomi's suggestion?
3. In what ways can relationships in general, and marriage in particular, strengthen our sense of identity?
4. What do you feel local churches can do to provide support for everyone within their church community whatever their individual status?

12

GETTING READY

Wash and perfume yourself, and put on your best clothes.
(Ruth 3:3)

READ: RUTH 3:3-5

It was an official-sounding job title: 'Decision-Maker'. It was also one which carried with it the power to affect welfare payments, and for a time I worked alongside members of such a team. This was a component in the network of support to help jobless benefit claimants find work. But it was a 'carrot-and-stick' approach. The negative element involved sanctions being applied for non-attendance at stipulated interviews and courses.

The 'carrot' aspect in giving help to the unemployed consisted of courses being free, 'hands-on' and aimed specifically at getting customers 'job-ready'. As well as giving advice on locating suitable vacancies, help in completion of application forms, and drawing up a CV (curriculum vitae – details of previous employment, education and qualifications). Assistance was also given in preparing for the all-important job interview. Techniques, answering questions and personal presentation were covered for this purpose.

FACT FINDING

Naomi's action in trying to find a place where Ruth might be *'well provided for'* (3:1) was also extremely thorough. A vital interview constituted a key part of this undertaking. She had carried out her research in an intensive fashion. Having already noted that Boaz was a kinsman-redeemer, being a close relative, she had realised something else. He had taken note of her daughter-in-law working in his field and had approached her in a kind and thoughtful way. His concern for her had included advice that she remain working in his field alongside his harvesters for protection. This not only marked Boaz out as someone with financial resources that would enable him to carry out the necessary purchase of Naomi's land (to 'redeem' it) but confirmed his godly attitude that was on a par with Naomi's and Ruth's.

However, Naomi had done more than pick up this background, though essential, information. On the basis of these details she had taken a further step. She had discerned a means by which Ruth could approach him and, with no one else around, highlight his obligation as a kinsman-redeemer. Boaz was tracked down in order for this to be carried out. *'Tonight he will be winnowing barley on the threshing-floor'* (3:2). So Ruth was instructed to *'note the place'* where he had settled, before going to uncover his feet and lying down. Then, having taken that action, she was simply told, *'He will tell you what to do'* (3:4). Those last words were possibly spoken more in hope than expectation!

RUTH'S ROLE

Those directions to Ruth regarding her eventual encounter with Boaz that night were not given in isolation. They were preceded by a very clear series of commands: '*Wash and perfume yourself, and put on your best clothes*' (3:3). Whilst Ruth's subsequent steps were to end up with her taking a leap of faith – Boaz's response to her unexpected presence and (basically) a request for marriage could not be guaranteed – here was something that she could undertake (and needed to do) in order to contribute to the outcome. Like preparing for a job interview, the homework of possible scenarios and ensuring a suitable personal appearance needed to be undertaken.

> ...a part which we have to play...

God's work and the directions that He wants us to take may lead us into situations where we have to go out 'on a limb'. But there will always be a part which we have to play in what takes place, even (dare that word be used) if it only involves fervent prayer! As with Ruth, however, God may require us to take some tangible and practical action that's within our grasp. Ruth was ready to receive the advice and support of her mother-in-law and act on it. It's likely that God will place people alongside us who will be able to offer wisdom and insight as well as prayer support. We need to be alert to connections and networks which God may have provided to facilitate steps for our spiritual growth.

So what did Naomi say to Ruth that relates to us? All the other events that had previously taken place were important. But they tended to be governed by force of circumstances and opting for the obvious. God was undoubtedly behind those events but now a more proactive stance was necessary.

WASHED

The first of these steps that Ruth had to take was to '*Wash*' (3:3). No doubt there was a practical reason for this action. Hygiene, both general and personal, is necessary to combat disease and prevent the spread of bacteria. When human proximity is required then this is particularly important. Failure to pay attention to this basic care can give out an unintended message! In Ruth's case, her labour in the heat of the day certainly needed remedying. But she also couldn't approach Boaz looking and smelling like Moab, her place of origin. There may have been aspects of Ruth's previous spiritual experiences and environment arising from her culture and lifestyle which clung to her. These now had no place in her new life in Israel. They needed to be washed away, physically and spiritually.

The biblical context of 'washing' is often presented in relation to sin. Naaman, afflicted with leprosy (a picture of spiritual uncleanness) was told to *'wash'* himself in the River Jordan in order to receive healing (see 2 Kings 5). The psalmist prayed that God would *'Wash'* away his *'iniquity'* (Psalm 51:2). The apostle Paul described being approached by a disciple of Jesus just days following his Damascus Road conversion and being told: *'Get up, be baptised and wash your sins away...'* (Acts 22:16). Paul was clearly already a Christian at this point, but baptism (total immersion) was not only a sign and testimony to what had taken place, but also a means of opening up a spiritual future. This was expounded in his letter to Christians in Rome: *'We were therefore buried with him through baptism into death in order that, just as Christ was raised from the dead through the glory of the Father, we too may live a new life'* (Romans 6:4). It was this baptism into new life by faith, *'...*

> ...drew a spiritual line in her life.

no longer [being] *slaves to sin'* (Romans 6:6), which was portrayed in the Old Testament by washing.

Ruth, like Paul many centuries later, was already a believer in God. But this action of 'washing' was an outward act which drew a spiritual line in her life. Deep-seated scars arising from her previous experiences, the effects of which may have been lingering in Ruth's heart and spirit, could now be put away. Her more distant, as well as recent past, which had marred her God-gifted identity could now be viewed as having been washed away in order to safeguard her future. The same can be true for ourselves in terms of baptism.

ANOINTED

However, it was not sufficient for Ruth to wash, she also then needed to *'perfume'* (3:3) herself (*'anoint'*, KJV). She had not only to remove all vestiges of dirt, physical and spiritual, but to replace it. Scented oils were to be applied. A pleasant aroma would now surround her. This was not just for the benefit of other people but a reminder to herself that she had experienced a difference which was both outward and deep within. The apostle Paul stated that '... *we are ... the fragrance of life...*' (2 Corinthians 2:16). The psalmist underlined this action contributing to a growing sense of change in a person's life and identity: '*I shall be anointed with fresh oil*' (Psalm 92:10, KJV), oil also being a picture of God's Holy Spirit who initially comes upon us at conversion.

Further, the Old Testament accounts describing the call of Israel's first two kings, Saul and then David, featured these aspects in relation to identity. Both of these men were anointed with oil (by the prophet Samuel). They both then experienced God's Holy Spirit coming upon them, empowering them and marking out their leadership role.

CLOTHED

There was further action which Ruth needed to take before stepping out into the unknown of that 'interview' with Boaz. She needed to put on her 'best clothes' (3:3). This was not a show of ostentation or means of being seductive. It was both to indicate respect and parity with him as their subsequent conversation was to show. Other biblical examples provide a similar outlook. Joseph was dramatically released from prison when it was discovered that he could interpret dreams. But in being presented to Pharaoh, the one who had suffered nightmares, he needed to have 'changed his clothes' (Genesis 41:14). The parable of the prodigal son included the command from the father to 'Bring the best robe and put it on him' (Luke 15:22). The lesser known parable of the wedding feast recorded the detail of a guest being put out of the banquet because he failed to wear the appropriate clothing (Matthew 22:11–13). The prophet Isaiah wrote of us having 'filthy rags' (64:6) but now being 'arrayed' in a 'robe of righteousness' (Isaiah 61:10). In God's perspective we are now declared as clean and enabled to have a close relationship with him.

Those clothes which Ruth now wore indicated a similar significant change in her life. She had trusted in the God of Israel, putting away foreign gods and associated practices. In putting on these clothes she had indicated her new life in God. This had also shown her sense of significance and value – her real identity gifted by God. Paul in the New Testament described this as now being 'in Christ' and being a 'new creation; the old has gone, the new has come' (2 Corinthians 5:17). Further, Ruth's bold statement and request soon to be directed to Boaz revealed an additional change in her perception. Whatever shame – worthlessness and pollution – that might have been generated by her previous lifestyle had also now been symbolically put away. The psalmist had been acutely aware of this powerful feeling being dealt with by reason of his relationship with God when he declared: 'No-one whose hope is in you will ever be put to shame...' (Psalm 25:3).

READY

All these outward and spiritually symbolic acts were to be taken a stage further when she approached Boaz that night requesting that he 'Spread' the corner of his garment over her. For both of them there were spiritual and emotional connotations in what was about to take place.

Ruth was now ready for that 'interview'. The next step of her life was soon to be determined. But the outcome was not in her own hands, nor those of Boaz, but in God's. However, like ourselves, Ruth needed to prepare and to have a growing sensitivity as to her identity.

FOR REFLECTION

1. What changes do you think Ruth felt when she undertook these three actions?
2. Why can these actions be such a powerful picture of our own inner spiritual change, including dealing with shame?
3. What effect does it have on our relationship with God when we know that we are clean in His sight?
4. Why is it important to be aware that our marred and damaged identity, arising from sin, can be changed by the fact that we have become a 'new creation'?

13

DARKNESS

Tonight he will be winnowing barley on the threshing-floor.
(Ruth 3:2)

READ: RUTH 3: 6–15

'Darkness' and 'night-time' do not project very positive images. They are often associated with emotive terms such as 'fear', 'vulnerability', threatening' and 'danger'. Our automatic response is therefore to try to generate light or brightness. History records some grim periods of political and social darkness. Winston Churchill, the prime minister of Great Britain during the Second World War, made many awe-inspiring speeches at that time, including one regarding this being the nation's 'finest hour'. Given in the summer of 1940 when the country faced the horrors of Hitler's Nazi Party, it included a phrase which encapsulated such a terrible prospect, 'the abyss of a new dark age'.

However, there was an even blacker day in the history of this world when Jesus Christ was crucified. Matthew's Gospel recorded of that occasion: *'From the sixth hour until the ninth hour darkness came over all the land.'* This was not simply physical but also spiritual. *'About the ninth hour Jesus cried out in a loud voice, "Eloi, Eloi, lama sabachthani?" – which means, "My God, my God, why have you forsaken me?"'* (Matthew 27:45,46).

THE UNKNOWN

The blackness of Calvary was prefigured many centuries earlier. This was when the Children of Israel were slaves in Egypt and God appointed Moses to bring about their escape – the Exodus. This was only achieved following God's angel of death going through the land and striking down the firstborn of every family. The exception was those households whose doorframes were coated with the blood of a lamb that had been killed in accordance with God's instructions. This was the Passover, and it took place at night. Like the events on that hill outside Jerusalem, the darkness also presented a picture of the uncertainty (from a human perspective) of both what was happening and the outcome.

This was also the situation when those escaping Israelites reached the Red Sea on the road out of Egypt. Again it was night-time. Hotly pursued by Pharaoh and his army, the future again was totally unknown. But then, *'... all that night the LORD drove the sea back with a strong east wind and turned it into dry land'* (Exodus 14:21). The Israelites crossed over to safety, but the Egyptian army was drowned by the returning waters when they tried to follow them.

STEPPING OUT IN DARKNESS

But what of Ruth? Night-time was also the designated period for her to step out. This was in the direction that her mother-in-law had pointed. Even though much in her life had changed, she was still in a place of being a foreigner in a strange land, a widow, childless, poor, having a pagan background and needing to toil in a stranger's field. Although in a spiritual sense she had taken 'refuge' under the 'wings' of the God of Israel (2:12), this had not made any substantial impact on her life in an outward way. Many of us are like Ruth, with ongoing 'baggage' seemingly still clinging to us.

So Ruth is someone with whom many of us can identify. Like her we may still be looking for a place to 'settle', a purpose in life and sense of real identity. But for the moment we are in darkness, uncertainty and vulnerability. It was into such 'darkness' that Ruth was now required to step alone.

In that context with, humanly speaking, the odds stacked against success, she followed the instructions of her mother-in-law: 'I will do whatever you say' (3:5). A number of outcomes were possible. At best she could be rebuffed by Boaz, or he might simply not understand what she wanted. It could be that Boaz failed to recognise her at all, his kindness to her in the past being something that he had now forgotten. At worst, she could be accused of attempted seduction, with the associated threat of losing her livelihood, severing of relationships, ejection from the land of Israel or even capital punishment. Her resolve and sheer courage must have been mixed with deep apprehension within an already bruised and battered heart in this environment of darkness and an unknown outcome.

...with deep apprehension...

Meanwhile the unsuspecting Boaz had, as Naomi stated, gone down to the threshing floor. The actual reason for him being there is not known. Perhaps it was to guard the grain from theft, or to enable him to achieve a full day's work without time and energy being spent going home. Or it could have been in his role as an employer that he stayed on-site, wanting to be around when the first 'shift' appeared in order to encourage and monitor their efforts.

DISTURBED SLEEP

'*So* [Ruth] *went down*' to the place where Boaz lay, the location being on a lower elevation of the town, and '*uncovered his feet*' (3:6,7). She then lay down herself, almost certainly by Boaz's feet as distinct from his side. And, in that darkness, she waited. That was as important as everything else that she had done. She had prepared herself, followed Naomi's instructions, walked down to the threshing floor at night-time, and approached the sleeping Boaz '*quietly*' (3:7). It was now up to God.

Waking people during the night or disturbing their sleep with vivid dreams seems to be quite a common 'tool' used by God! The latter was experienced by high-profile despots such as Pharaoh (at the time of Joseph) and Nebuchadnezzar (at the time of Daniel). A further national leader, King Xerxes, the Persian potentate, could not sleep on one occasion and so ordered the government records to be read aloud to him. This proved a vital link in the chain for Esther, another sensitive woman like Ruth, to make herself vulnerable and be used by God in a significant way.

As with the Xerxes, Scripture is not specific in describing the actual reason for Boaz's sleep being broken, whether it was directly due to God, or something else. The original Hebrew meaning of the word used to describe him as being '*startled*' (3:8) is unclear, according to experts. The only thing that we need to know is that Ruth, having positioned herself at his feet, waited for something to happen... and it did!

RUTH'S REPLY

A question immediately comes from Boaz's lips when he awakes and, it seems, straightaway recognises a woman lying at his feet: *'Who are you?'* (3:9) It's been previously noted that the majority of this biblical book is made up of conversations, including key questions. Boaz, having some time previously asked, *'Whose young woman is that?'* (2:5) was now asking this further one. But he was no longer in a field where Ruth was a nobody amongst a crowd of other people gleaning to make ends meet. This was just Ruth and Boaz, alone and secluded. And Ruth's response was vital in terms of what happened next. Having previously been described in the narrative as being *'Ruth the Moabitess'* (see 1:22; 2:2; 2:21), she simply answered on this occasion, *'I am your servant Ruth'* (3:9). The baggage of her past, her shame and identity bound up in that term *'Moabitess'* was gone. She was now simply *'Ruth'* and *'your servant'*. This was in contrast to her earlier reply in which she had confessed that she did not have *'the standing of one of your servant girls'* (2:13). Her sense of identity based upon her relationship with God was beginning to emerge.

> The baggage of her past... was gone.

But Ruth did not restrict herself simply to answering Boaz's question. At this point she went seriously 'off-script'. The request that she then put to Boaz had not appeared in those careful instructions from Naomi... but did seem inspired by God! It was also indicative of her growing sense of significance. She picked up on that previous commendation made by Boaz at their first meeting, *'May you be richly rewarded by the LORD, the God of Israel, under whose wings you have come to take refuge'* (2:12) and connected that word, *'wings'* with *'corner of your garment'*. Perhaps with almost a hint of boldness (and faith) she made her 'unscripted' request: *'Spread the corner of your garment over me, since you are a kinsman-redeemer'* (3:9).

THE RESPONSE

Was there a pause between Ruth uttering those words which could not now be retrieved, and Boaz answering? Did he need time to digest what had been said in order to respond? The words that had been spoken were important. *'[C]orner of your garment'*, together with that previous one, *'wings'*, were both pictures in respect of 'protection'. The former was used by the prophet Ezekiel meaning a request for marriage (*'I spread the corner of my garment over you'*, Ezekiel 16:8).

Boaz's response highlighted some particular features. The first is that he recognised God as being involved in all aspects of his life, even at night-time with this foreign widow. He used the term, *'The LORD bless you'* (3:10), which was similar to the greeting to his employees back in the field when he first noticed Ruth. His response was to echo that at the end: *'... as the LORD lives...'* (3:13) Secondly, it revealed that he was no longer a young man but still unmarried. Whether he was a widower, unable to find a spiritually compatible wife in those days when there had been a general turning from God, or being on account of his mother being a foreigner with a 'past' (Rahab, as previously noted) which made him in some way unsuitable for marriage, was not explained.

Perhaps there was a tinge of poignancy in his reply to Ruth in that she could have *'run after'* (3:10) younger men if she had chosen to do so, either on account of their wealth or attraction. As Boaz implied, she was still a younger person herself, able to be a mother in due course. Their age difference seemed underlined by Boaz's use of the term, *'my daughter'* (3:11). The third element of his reply emerged in the comment he added to those tender words. This related to how others viewed her: '*All my fellow townsmen know that you are a woman of noble character*' (3:11). Was Ruth aware of that reputation? Possibly not, since if she or Naomi had known how she was viewed then this extraordinarily risky approach might have been supplanted by a more conventional course of action. But again it contributed to her sense of identity.

KINSMAN-REDEEMER

There was a final element in Boaz's response to Ruth. He specifically picked up the basis of her request in him being a kinsman-redeemer with the associated responsibility to act. However, there was a problem. Boaz sensitively picked up and 'ran' with Ruth's request, calming her anxiety by prefacing his readiness to act with, '*don't be afraid*' (3:11). But then he pointed out that there was another kinsman-redeemer who was '*nearer*' (3:12) than himself. Had Naomi failed to identify this other man as being a closer relative? More importantly, had God not been aware of this fact?

But God's plans are not thwarted, whatever the outward circumstances. Boaz certainly was not giving up easily! Although his words seemed to indicate that he was not bothered if this other kinsman-redeemer took up the option of redemption, the account that follows shows otherwise. Boaz was both astute and determined. He was not only resolute in sorting out this matter on the basis of Ruth's request but also because he had recognised her clear faith in God,.

PROVISION

Boaz's sensitivity towards Ruth was revealed in two further ways as this scene closed. He directed Ruth to remain at the threshing floor. The narrative was precise about the fact that '*she lay at his feet until morning'* (3:14). Then, when it was sufficiently light for her to safely make her way back home, but not so clear so that she would be recognised, she departed. Boaz was keen to ensure that her reputation was not put at risk and there was no damage to her sense of identity. He was also making sure that she was not in peril of physical attack on account of being outside at night.

But he also took further action to show his care and practical provision that additionally pointed to the future. He poured into her shawl *'six measures of barley'* (3:15), an amount that was both generous and manageable, food for the coming days. If he had failed to specifically *'Spread the corner'* of his garment over Ruth, this action, with regard to a part of her own clothing, provided a physical link with that request... and a sign to assure Naomi (as well as Ruth) that he was prepared to act as required by the law by way of a kinsman-redeemer. The waiting that Ruth had to experience when first approaching Boaz during that night was not yet over; she was going to have to do some more.

FOR REFLECTION

1. What feelings might arise when we are in circumstances that are 'dark'?

2. Why is it hard to trust God and 'step out' in such circumstances?

3. Why is it important to remember the fact of our relationship with God when stepping out in faith?

4. Why is it important not to panic when things don't seem to work out after we take steps seemingly directed by God?

14

WAITING...
AGAIN

Then Naomi said, 'Wait, my daughter, until you find out what happens.
For the man will not rest until the matter is settled today.'
(Ruth 3:18)

READ: RUTH 3:16–18

The story is told of a theology professor who was found in an agitated state, pacing up and down his study. When asked what the trouble was, he replied: 'The trouble is that I'm in a hurry, but God is not!'

Many of us can identify with that comment, at least some of the time. The drive to get things done, actively press on and not hang around is commonplace. Instant communications and technological innovation in widespread use adds impetus to this urge. Being proactive and hands-on is seen, even in church life, as being a vital attribute.

CHANGING GEAR

This account of Ruth had seen her having this proactive stance with regard to her approaching and speaking to Boaz. Yet now we come to a point where she was specifically told to '*Wait*' (3:18). This instruction as with the one concerning the need to take preparatory action in washing, anointing and clothing herself, came from her mother-in-law. The latter was clearly sensitive to what was taking place both on the surface but also in the spiritual realm. Knowing when to 'change gear' was particularly important at this delicate stage. Naomi realised that now was the moment for Ruth not to do anything except wait.

However, this had not been an isolated occasion. In the unfolding events described in this book, there had been other key times when the principle characters had needed to hold back and simply wait for things to happen. Naomi herself had needed to remain away in Moab following the devastating loss of her husband and then her two sons, waiting for news of any change in the famine situation back home. Having eventually come back to Israel, she then had to await Ruth's return from her first day of gleaning in the fields amongst the leftovers to find out how she had got on, and where she had actually worked. As we have just seen, Ruth had subsequently needed to wait in the vicinity of the threshing floor to find out where Boaz was going to be lying down before she could approach him, needing to also wait for him then to awake from sleep.

REASONS TO WAIT

Most of these periods of waiting were quite brief. Indeed, this further one was also going to be short. But it needed to be done. If, for any reason, Ruth had chosen to force the issue of marriage and the responsibility of undertaking the obligation of kinsman-redeemer, she would most likely have undone all that had been accomplished so far. If she had approached the other, unnamed, relative, she would have no certainty of the outcome and could have been easily rebuffed or ignored by him. This was particularly likely on account of this man's character, which was to emerge. A further option was of approaching the other elders of the city, before whom Boaz had to undertake his negotiations with this other man. However, if she had tried to put her case in order for to achieve a favourable outcome, she would almost certainly have been repelled, since this was a matter on an official level entirely between the two kinsman-redeemers.

But just as Ruth had listened to Naomi on those previous occasions, so she did again. Perhaps at this stage it was increasingly obvious that everything was in the hands of God and that he was working through the actions of Boaz. As far as mother and daughter-in-law were concerned, this was now outside their influence. They knew that Boaz was following through on his promise, but that even he could not guarantee fulfilment in terms of him redeeming (or buying) Naomi's land and responding to Ruth's request for marriage.

> ...everything was in the hands of God...

RELIANCE

Similar experiences may arise in our lives when we need to respond to what is happening (or not happening) to us or around us by simply waiting. The drive to act and attempt to influence events has to be pushed to one side. But this act of waiting is not with the attitude of vaguely hoping that something might happen, or being laid-back without any sense of care or responsibility. Neither of these attitudes were applicable to Naomi or Ruth. Instead, like them, there needs to be a trusting reliance upon God and what He has promised. Naomi has stressed that Boaz would not 'rest' (3:18). We can also be reassured that God will not be ignorant of our situations or powerless to intervene. The psalmist described his attitude as follows: '*I am still confident of this: I will see the goodness of the LORD in the land of the living. Wait for the LORD; be strong and take heart and wait for the LORD*' (Psalm 27:13,14).

MOTIVES

There is a further reason for needing to wait. Not only does it focus our reliance upon God, but it can also bring hidden motives to the surface, both our own and those of people around us. On one occasion the psalmist prayed that God would forgive his '*hidden faults*', and on another: '*Search me, O God, and know my heart; test me and know my anxious thoughts. See if there is any offensive way in me, and lead me in the way everlasting*' (Psalm 19:12; 139:23,24). When nothing seems to be happening, there can be space for us to examine ourselves and ask serious questions which we would not otherwise consider.

PERSPECTIVE

Similarly, the act of waiting can help us put things into perspective, especially in understanding God's work in our lives. The writer of Lamentations had watched in horror as events around him unfolded. The nation of Israel was being subjected to atrocities to which God did not seem to respond. As his emotions went into overdrive he realised that his view of the situation was out of focus. In an effort to concentrate on God, he wrote: '*Yet this I call to mind and therefore I have hope: Because of the LORD'S great love we are not consumed, for his compassions never fail. They are new every morning; great is your faithfulness. I say to myself: "The LORD is my portion; therefore I will wait for him." The LORD is good to those whose hope is in him, to the one who seeks him; it is good to wait quietly for the salvation of the LORD. It is good for a man to bear the yoke while he is young*'

(3:21–27). Both Naomi and Ruth had experienced this goodness of God against the backdrop of deep hurt and vulnerability. This waiting helped them put things into perspective and anticipate his intervention again, even though circumstances meant that they were helpless. Reflecting upon God's previous work in our lives can, in such moments of waiting, also enable us to have a better perspective on God's love and power.

SPACE

Lastly, waiting gives God the space to work in a miraculous way. Our ego and self-confidence can lead us to believe that we can contribute to what God is doing in

...waiting for God and trusting...

difficult situations. There may be an element for which we have to take responsibility. But there are also times when we need to step back and depend entirely upon God. This means that our responsibility is simply that of waiting for God and trusting in Him as, essentially, Ruth and Naomi were doing.

The prophet Isaiah had many gut-wrenching experiences in his life as he exercised spiritual oversight in the nation of Judah. When the country was under threat and God seemed inactive, he wrote of needing to make space: *'I will wait for the LORD, who is hiding his face from the house of Jacob. I will put my trust in him'* (8:17). The benefits were subsequently described: *'Yet the LORD longs to be gracious to you; he rises to show you compassion. For the LORD is a God of justice. Blessed are all who wait for him'* (30:18).

God's blessing at Pentecost, when His Holy Spirit was poured out upon the disciples, had been preceded by the specific command of Jesus prior to His ascension. *'Do not leave Jerusalem, but wait for the gift my Father promised, which you have heard me speak about. For John baptised with water, but in a few days you will be*

111

baptised with the Holy Spirit' (Acts 1:4,5). It was only as the wider circle of disciples were both waiting – making space for God to work – and *'all together in one place'* (Acts 2:1) that the Holy Spirit came upon them.

PART OF LIFE

However competent our organisational or management skills, we will always find that waiting is an activity which we have to undertake. Much of this will be enforced and out of our control. But the example of Naomi and Ruth shows that this can be a positive element in our journey of faith in God. He is never fazed or powerless. Waiting is part of the process through which God works to highlight our identity as we trust in Him. Those words which Naomi had spoken to Ruth about Boaz are also applicable to God: *'... the man will not rest...'* (3:18)

FOR REFLECTION

1. Why do we find it so hard to wait?
2. Naomi had discerned that this point in the unfolding of events was when Ruth needed to wait. What factors should we take into account in deciding that waiting is appropriate for us?
3. What qualities about God are helpful in being able to wait?
4. How does the ability to wait reflect spiritual growth?

15

THE TOWN GATE

Then Boaz announced to the elders and all the people, 'Today you are witnesses that I have bought from Naomi all the property of Elimelech, Kilion and Mahlon. I have also acquired Ruth the Moabitess, Mahlon's widow, as my wife, in order to maintain the name of the dead with his property, so that his name will not disappear from among his family or from the town records...'
(Ruth 4:9,10)

READ: RUTH 4: 1–11

The sale of property around 1000BC in Israel didn't seem to be very different from the housing market activity today. The process itself may vary, but legal niceties and sums of money are common features. So are the emotional effects! Uncertainty, anxiety and frustration seem to be feelings that are experienced by the parties involved in this procedure, whatever the date on the calendar.

Technological advances seem to make no difference to this stress. When involved in the sale of my late mother's house, I received an unexpected email one afternoon from one of the solicitors who was involved in this transaction. After weeks of silence and seeming inactivity, the legal profession had suddenly sprung into life! I was caught up in this whirlwind of activity and required to deliver certain documentation to their offices – now! This was only accomplished by using old technology – a bicycle with me on it – racing into central London. A few days later, this whole process was repeated, albeit with different certification, showing that ineptitude by such professions was not an isolated occurrence. I was having to do the donkey work, but the solicitors' eventual bill for their services didn't seem to reflect this fact!

Fortunately, the steps needed to transfer ownership of property at the time of Naomi and Ruth seemed slightly less complicated. However, there were clearly defined actions that had to be undertaken. And uncertainty was still a factor.

THE OTHER KINSMAN

In this process, the spotlight was now focused on Boaz. Naomi and Ruth could only wait for the outcome. In order for him to carry out his role as kinsman-redeemer, he needed to approach the man who was a closer relative. This other, unnamed, man had a better claim in purchasing the land that belonged to Naomi now that her husband and both sons were dead. Up to this point, the fact that Naomi owned such property had been entirely absent from the narrative. In one sense it was irrelevant. The character and spiritual journeys of Naomi and Ruth, and then of Boaz, had been the important and dominant features. It is a tragedy of our own age that so much emphasis is placed on material resources and their acquisition. Relationships with people and God seem to trail behind.

But Naomi's property now emerged as a major factor in Ruth's 'journey' to a place where she could 'settle'. It seems very doubtful as to whether it was of any benefit. There were no male members of the immediate family left to cultivate it. So once the current harvest was over and Ruth could no longer glean, there was no other source of income, apart from the sale of this land. However, if such a sale was undertaken by a third party, someone outside the family, then the money raised from this transaction could only keep the women alive in the near future. The loss of this valuable asset as a means of generating income through its produce would result in poverty for them in time to come. But it also had other, more important, significance.

COMMUNITY AND LAND

The ownership (more properly described as 'stewardship') of land in that culture was not only a principal means of livelihood, but an aspect of life involving relationship within families and with God. It was God who had brought the Israelites into this Promised Land, giving them instructions through Moses in respect of it being divided up. Each tribe, clan and family was allocated specified pieces of land for use in supporting themselves. Under the leadership of Joshua, the conquest of this territory was carried out, at least in part, and God's directions were followed through.

Land constituted a tangible aspect of family and national identity. It also formed a 'connection' with God, on account of the produce grown on it being essential elements in the various annual feasts and associated offerings. Even in contemporary society there is acknowledgement that despite scientific advances in farming techniques, the productivity of the land is dependent upon 'nature' (for which we would read 'God'). Keeping land within family ownership was therefore integral to ongoing life in Israel, being the 'horizontal' or 'sideways' link with people in the family unit, as well as the 'vertical' one with God.

THE TOWN GATE

Naomi's confidence in Boaz was now to be shown as justified, as was her unstated but implied trust in God. Boaz, clearly being a man of his word, undertook the necessary legal proceedings. He first of all dealt with the obstacle that he had described to Ruth, the problem of a nearer relative who had first claim on purchasing Naomi's land.

So Boaz went to the open space by the gate of the town, a place where civic and legal matters were handled. He was probably one of the elders in that town and seemed to have sufficient authority to call his fellow leaders, following the arrival of the other kinsman-redeemer on the scene. This enabled Boaz to put to him the proposition of buying Naomi's land in his capacity as closest kinsman-redeemer. He agreed, seemingly without hesitation, to carry this out. It is possible that he was only aware of Naomi as being the relevant party in this situation, calculating that her age would make it impossible for her to raise up another heir for Elimelech (her late husband) and that the property would therefore have then reverted to him alone (and his family line).

This decision of that other kinsman-redeemer seemed to have destroyed the possibility of Boaz being able to marry Ruth in that capacity himself. Could he have married her anyway? Commentators on this Bible passage don't seem to address this question. But perhaps it would have been entirely inappropriate because of Ruth being a foreigner, significantly younger than him, and being much lower in the 'pecking order' of that culture.

AN ADDITIONAL CONDITION

But Boaz appeared entirely unfazed by this man's decision to buy Naomi's property. Perhaps he was inwardly smiling with quiet confidence. But perhaps, like Naomi when advising Ruth before she had approached him, he had also done some homework. He was aware that this other relative had existing family connections (he may have been

…he had also done some 'homework.'

married already) which he had not fully taken into account when responding to that initial proposition. So Boaz introduced the matter of an attached condition to such a purchase. 'Redeeming' (purchasing) Naomi's land also required marrying Ruth. This was in order to raise children and ensure that the property remained within, and safeguarding, Elimelech's family line. Boaz was pointing out that as kinsman-redeemer there was a duty which not only involved Naomi's two sons (to whom the land would otherwise have reverted in ownership) but now their widows. Only one of these (Ruth) was present in Bethlehem, but she now constituted the crucial element in this legal process.

This was not an issue of materialism and the drive to acquire possessions that was being discussed. Rather, it was the ownership of an essential resource for the maintenance of family life as God had ordained it. This aspect was specified, as with the regulations about land, in the Mosaic Law which laid down the provision of a brother marrying his dead brother's widow (see Deuteronomy 25:5,6).

A CHANGE OF MIND

With this new scenario concerning marriage to Ruth being raised, the unnamed man changed his mind. His explanation revealed, perhaps, something of his character. It may also have revealed a prejudice of others and lack of trust in God – Boaz had already shown that these were not part of his spiritual DNA. Boaz had clearly spelt out the fact that Ruth was a Moabitess and a widow, the latter implying that she was in poverty. Did this put the 'wind up' the other man? In response, perhaps with shuffling feet and eyes directed away from those elders, he said that going through with his initial decision would mean that he would *'endanger'* his own *'estate'* – *'I cannot do it'* (4:6). In effect he was saying that the necessary marriage to Ruth would mean that any resulting sons would eventually inherit that land, and this nearer kinsman's own family would not benefit from the purchase in the long run. He would be spending money that could ultimately lead to his own relatives losing out.

The man's agenda was revealed. He could not afford to take any risk of loss. He cared more for the material element than for providing care and protection to Ruth. But this opened the door for Boaz. The other kinsman, having waived his right, stepped out of the picture, but not before undertaking a sandal-removing routine to signify his final decision. Sadly this practice, much simpler and less expensive than our present legal transactions, is no longer part of the statutory process! So once again in accordance with the law he handed Boaz his sandal and confirmed his action with the words, *'Buy it yourself'* (4:8; see also Deuteronomy 25:7–10).

Boaz was therefore able to bring about the completion of this last part of Ruth's journey. His declaration before witnesses of buying Naomi's property and ensuring that it remained within that family circle by having Ruth as his wife was greeted by the response of affirmation from the elders and others at the town gate.

These events may have taken place in a completely different era from our own, and yet they are still relevant. Our own lives may seem, at least at times, to be entirely in the hands of other people so that we are powerless to make any difference or to effect any change. But Boaz is a picture of the God who intervenes and acts *'on behalf of those who wait for him'* (Isaiah 64:4). Our God-gifted identity and destiny is not down to what other people, known and unknown, say or do to us. Ultimately our lives are in the hands of God. This was why the psalmist was able to assert: *'But you are a shield around me, O Lord; you bestow glory on me and lift up my head. To the Lord I cry aloud, and he answers me from his holy hill'* (Psalm 3:3,4). Like Boaz, He spares no effort in working in every part of our lives to bring us to a place where we can *'settle'*... finding our God-given significance and value.

FOR REFLECTION

1. Why is there a tendency in modern society to place so much value on possessions?
2. In what way was the offering of produce from the land to God at the various Jewish feasts and festivals a helpful way of getting a better perspective on personal possessions and property being given by God?
3. How can a preoccupation with possessions be a barrier to finding our real significance and specialness?
4. How can we act in a more trusting way towards God with regard to our possessions?

16

SETTLING

*So Boaz took Ruth and she became his wife. ... and the Lord enabled
her to conceive, and she gave birth to a son.*

(Ruth 4:13)

READ: RUTH 4:9–22

The details on a Blue Plaque introduced us to the life of Ruth...
the subject of a further one draws our study of her journey to an
end. An unknown South African activist and writer was featured
in the first instance. But someone whose work was much better
known to Londoners was commemorated on this second plaque.
In addition to these memorials being sited on houses in the same
locality, the other common feature was that both of these men's
activities involved travel.

Solomon Plaaje's trek may simply have involved passing
through this city, but Harry Beck lived and worked in the capital. In
particular he was the designer of the iconic London Underground
map, now an essential tool for tourists and visitors. He was an
unemployed engineering draftsman when originally devising
it in 1931. In one sense it was not a proper map. The routes of

each Underground line are not straight, and the stations are not equidistant from each other. And the River Thames definitely does not follow those smooth contours as depicted on the map! But that was the inspiration behind his design. It meant that it was easy to read and to follow. A hassle-free journey across London could be clearly planned – in theory, at least!

RUTH'S 'MAP'

Ruth's journey in life, alongside Naomi, was one which we have seen as being more than physical and geographical. She was also travelling in a spiritual sense, her identity being interwoven with her deepening relationship with God. But in doing so she, together with her mother-in-law, was impacted by tragedy, uncontrolled change and ongoing uncertainty. These affected their emotions, perceptions, faith and self-worth.

The details of Ruth's experience in particular may be entirely different from our own. But living in the same sin-sick and spiritually darkened world we, like Ruth, her mother-in-law and those travellers described in Psalm 107 are liable to be afflicted by a lack of direction, wandering from God, and helplessness.

The knock-on effect of all of this was to warp and distort whatever view Ruth may have had of herself. The 'map' of her life was a mess, if it existed at all. We can probably identify with those feelings, together with the difficulty in finding our God-gifted identity, a place to 'settle'.

GOD'S WORK

As we have also seen as we have explored Ruth's experiences alongside Naomi, God had been working. Interestingly, this Old Testament book makes no reference to any of these three major characters, Ruth, Naomi or Boaz, actually praying to God. (At least this is not so intriguing an omission as that of the book of Esther, which makes no reference at all to God!) However, the relationship which each of them had with God could not, on account of their lifestyle and attitude, be doubted. This relationship was also clear from the way in which God worked in their lives behind the scenes so that Ruth was eventually brought to the place of marriage and motherhood.

Being part of community – a spiritual 'family' as well as a biological one, as Ruth eventually experienced – can be key factors in recognising our God-gifted identity and purpose. The latter was clearly marked out for Ruth in terms of her giving birth to a son who was to be the grandfather of Israel's greatest king, David. It also meant that she, alongside some other very unlikely candidates, was in the line of human ancestors leading up to the birth of the Lord Jesus.

Whilst not all of us – if many at all – will have such a clear and prominent purpose as Ruth, we are all to be part of God's work in building His kingdom. And our part is unique and special; we are God's *'workmanship, created in Christ Jesus to do good works, which God prepared in advance for us to do'* (Ephesians 2:10). And our sense of identity is an essential element in that work, both in respect of equipping us to fulfil those *'works'*, and being strengthened as we undertake it.

> ...our part is unique and special...

PROPHETIC BLESSING

There was, however, an important element described in the closing verses of this narrative, which also added to Ruth's awareness of her identity... and will also add to our own. The immediate response of the elders and others who were around when Boaz announced his intention of marrying Ruth was to pronounce a blessing upon her: '*May the* LORD *make the woman who is coming into your home like Rachel and Leah, who together built up the house of Israel*' (4:11).

Those words were reflecting on the work of God that had been experienced in the past. They were now being applied to someone in the present. Whilst the exact events were not duplicated – as far as we know, Ruth only had the one child, whereas Rachel and Leah had a combined total of twelve (!) – the sense of blessing and giving birth on account of God's intervention was the underlying thread. This was the perspective that God had on this current situation. The 'prophetic word' inevitably involves a reminder being brought of something that God is recorded in the Bible as having said or done, and applying it into the present.

The prophetic word brought by the elders and others was then spoken over Boaz. A different aspect of God's work in the past was highlighted for this purpose: '*Through the offspring the* LORD *gives you by this young woman, may your family be like that of Perez, whom Tamar bore to Judah*' (4:12). Perez was actually Boaz's ancestor, a result of a union very loosely and unintentionally based on the practice of a brother marrying the widow of his deceased brother, and therefore having some similarity with Boaz's action. (For further details of the somewhat sordid affair regarding Tamar, see Genesis 38.) The descendants of Perez had raised the tribe of Judah to prominence in the nation of Israel. So the starting point of this blessing, '*May you have standing in Ephrathah and be famous in Bethlehem*' (4:11) was also in line with what God had done in the past.

NAOMI'S BLESSING

Naomi followed Ruth and Boaz in receiving a prophetic blessing. This took place some time later when Ruth had become a mother.

The women of the town declared to her: *'Praise be to the* LORD, *who this day has not left you without a kinsman-redeemer. May he become famous throughout Israel! He will renew your life and sustain you in your old age. For your daughter-in-law, who loves you and who is better to you than seven sons, has given him birth'* (4:14,15). Although not specifically referring back to God's previous intervention in the nation's history, it reflected God's heart of bringing blessing upon His people.

There were two aspects of this final blessing that were important. Both of them would have also impacted Ruth in terms of her identity. Firstly, her son was seen as sustaining Naomi in her *'old age'*. Assuming that Naomi was not, it seems, particularly old at this point, it indicated that Ruth's son would grow up into manhood. This eventuality was not to be taken for granted. Even up to a few generations ago in our own history, infant mortality was commonplace, and death on account of disease or frailty could be experienced at any age. Ruth had experienced this first-hand. Secondly, Ruth herself was viewed as being *'better ... than seven sons'*. Since the number 'seven' was considered a number denoting completeness, having seven sons was the epitome of all family blessings in Israel. Put simply, Ruth had surpassed the worth of seven sons to Naomi, the ultimate tribute in that culture.

SUPREME BLESSING

Whilst this particular blessing may have seemed over the top, it actually anticipated the amazing fact (as seen by God) that on account of Ruth, Naomi had become more than a grandmother (or even mother, since it was recorded in verse 17, *'Naomi has a son'*). She was to be the honoured ancestor of Israel's future leading family. Ruth had been someone who might have been viewed as simply 'tagging along' with Naomi when the latter returned to

Bethlehem. Now she was prophetically declared as the source of supreme blessing to her mother-in-law. Those women then, it seemed, even took on the responsibility of naming Naomi's grandson, giving him the name 'Obed', which meant 'servant' (possibly 'servant of the Lord').

GOD'S PERSPECTIVE

God still speaks into our lives and situations to bring His perspective on what is happening. Whether or not such prophetic expression is through other people underlining or drawing out a particular biblical verse or passage, it is important as a means by which we also receive 'strengthening, encouragement and comfort' (1 Corinthians 14:3). The apostle Paul also warned that prophecy was not to be treated 'with contempt' (1 Thessalonians 5:19). Although this account in Ruth does not describe any further events in Ruth's life, the raising of her son could have been fraught and difficult, particularly considering the spiritual environment in Israel at that time. Peer pressure and dysfunctional families are not confined to the twenty-first

...underlined in those prophetic blessings...

century! So for Ruth to have these clear declarations of God's perspective on her journey and the place to which she had now been brought was vital. Her specialness, significance and purpose had been underlined in those prophetic blessings, and pointed to an assured future. God continues to speak His words which are 'spirit and they are life' (John 6:63).

God had worked in Ruth's life, alongside Naomi, to come to a stage in her journey where she had fulfilled God's purpose for her. This had seemed entirely unlikely when the narrative first mentioned her. But her response to God and following through His directions enabled her not only to arrive in Israel to become the eventual ancestor of Jesus, but also to find her particular God-gifted identity, a place to 'settle'... an awareness which God wants for each of us.

FOR REFLECTION

1. To what degree do you see your life as a 'map', and how clearly is it marked out?

2. How important is it to have a sense of God-given purpose in our lives?

3. What is the value of hearing God's prophetic word or blessing?

4. How can we put ourselves in situations whereby we hear God's prophetic word or blessing?

APPENDIX

AFFIRMING OUR GOD-GIFTED IDENTITY

This exploration of the Book of Ruth has not been designed as an exhaustive study. It's certainly not intended as academic! Instead it has tried to unpack how God makes us aware of our personal identity. We have seen that circumstances and relationships were instrumental in God developing that awareness within Ruth's life. The words which were spoken to her, audible and unsaid, are also the means to impact us. That's why reading and pondering God's words in the Bible is so important.

The verses shown below provide a flavour of what God says to us. They have mainly been selected on the basis of personal experience – being invaluable in understanding how God sees me and his purposes in my life. But I'm still a 'work-in-progress'! So I shall still be reading these passages alongside you if, hopefully, you're able to make time to use them.

They are divided into groups of seven (one for each day of the week), placed under four broad headings, a framework in understanding our identity. As God speaks to us through them we, too, may be pointed to a place where we can, '*settle*'.

SIGNIFICANT

'Though my father and mother forsake me, the Lord will receive me.'
(Psalm 27:10)

*'You have not handed me over to the enemy but have
set my feet in a spacious place'*
(Psalm 31:8)

*'My frame was not hidden from you when I was made in the secret
place. When I was woven together in the depths of the earth, your
eyes saw my unformed body.'*
(Psalm 139:15, 16)

*But now, this is what the LORD says – he who created you, O Jacob, he
who formed you, O Israel: "Fear not, for I have redeemed you; I have
summoned you by name; you are mine."*
(Isaiah 43:1)

*'See, I have engraved you on the palms of my hands;
your walls are ever before me.'*
(Isaiah 49:16)

*'In him we were also chosen, having been predestined according to
the plan of him who works out everything in conformity with the
purpose of his will, in order that we, who were the first to hope in
Christ, might be for the praise of his glory'.*
(Ephesians 1:11-12)

'Consequently, you are no longer foreigners and aliens, but fellow-citizens with God's people and members of God's household.'
(Ephesians 2:19)

SPECIAL

'He brought me out into a spacious place; he rescued me because he delighted in me.'
(Psalm 18:19)

'Who redeems your life from the pit and crowns you with love and compassion, who satisfies your desires with good things so that your youth is renewed like the eagle's.'
(Psalm 103:4-5)

'For I am the LORD, your God, who takes hold of your right hand and says to you, "Do not fear; I will help you."'
(Isaiah 41:13)

'I have loved you with an everlasting love; I have drawn you with loving-kindness.'
(Jeremiah 31:3)

'I no longer call you servants, because a servant does not know his master's business. Instead, I have called you friends, for everything that I learned from my Father I have made known to you.'
(John 15:15)

'But because of his great love for us, God, who is rich in mercy, made us alive with Christ even when we were dead in transgressions – it is by grace you have been saved.'
(Ephesians 2:4-5)

'How great is the love the Father has lavished on us, that we should be called children of God! And that is what we are!'
(1 John 3:1)

SECURE

'Lord, you have assigned me my portion and my cup; you have made my lot secure. The boundary lines have fallen for me in pleasant places; surely I have a delightful inheritance.'
(Psalm 16: 5-6)

'I will instruct you and teach you in the way you should go; I will counsel you and watch over you.'
(Psalm 32:8)

'The Lord Almighty is with us; the God of Jacob is our fortress.'
(Psalm 46:11)

'He will not let your foot slip – he who watches over you will not slumber; indeed, he who watches over Israel will neither slumber nor sleep.'
(Psalm 121:3-4)

'The Lord will keep you from all harm – he will watch over your life; the Lord will watch over your coming and going both now and for evermore.'
(Psalm 121:7-8)

'So do not fear, for I am with you; do not be dismayed, for I am your God. I will strengthen you and help you; I will uphold you with my righteous right hand.'
(Isaiah 41:10)

'… because God has said, "Never will I leave you; never will I forsake you'"
(Hebrews 13:5)

SERVING

'The LORD will fulfill his purpose for me; your love, O LORD, endures forever – do not abandon the works of your hands.'
(Psalm 138:8)

"'For I know the plans I have for you," declares the LORD, "plans to prosper you and not to harm you, plans to give you hope and a future.'"
(Jeremiah 29:11)

'For we are God's fellow-workers; you are God's field, God's building.'
(1 Corinthians 3:9)

'For we are God's workmanship, created in Christ Jesus to do good works, which God   prepared in advance for us to do.'
(Ephesians 2:10)

'Being confident of this, that he who began a good work in you will carry it on to completion until the day of Christ Jesus.'
(Philippians 1:6)

'For it is God who works in you to will and to act according
to his good purpose.'
(Philippians 2:13)

'Whatever you do, work at it with all your heart, as working for the
Lord, not for men, since you know that you will receive an inheritance
from the Lord as a reward. It is the Lord Christ you are serving.'
(Colossians 3:23-24)

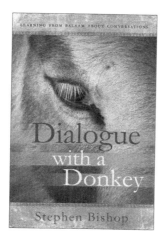

DIALOGUE WITH A DONKEY

Learning from Balaam about conversations

Stephen Bishop

A talking donkey and sword-wielding angel are the images most commonly associated with the Old Testament character of Balaam. Yet the significance and relevance of this account seem to be rarely considered.

"Dialogue with a Donkey" aims to open up this extraordinary story by looking at other conversations that were taking place... and which continue to do so. The compelling force of words to specifically direct, challenge, influence, affirm and develop people's lives are considered through Balaam's successive utterances. These pronouncements brought a divine perspective to the Israelites at that time. As this book advocates, we also need to hear what God is saying, breaking through all surrounding voices. It also underlines how Balaam's words reached a climax in pointing to Jesus who continues powerfully speaking into our darkness.

The stubborn donkey ends up being the means by which other people had God's life-giving word brought to them. We also need to hear such words. Are we listening?

ISBN 9781909824256
5.5 x 8.5" Paperback
Published by Zaccmedia

FLEECES, FEARS AND FLAMES

Gideon – Learning to connect with God

Stephen Bishop

Gideon is a well-known Bible character. His exploits in leading just three hundred men to defeat a huge invading army has inspired many people when faced with situations which are 'against-all-odds'. But how did it occur? Where was God in this scenario? How does this account relate to us?

'Fleeces, fears and flames' explores the Book of Judges in order to examine these ques-tions. Written in a down-to-earth manner, it looks at God connecting with Gideon despite his fears and fleece-laying doubts, then breaking through such frailty to release his power as seen in those flames. But it also shows that God is able to connect and work in our lives however daunting the challenges confronting us!

Suitable for individual reflection or group discussion, this material includes questions and a focus at the end of each main chapter to help connect the Biblical narrative in a personal way.

ISBN 9781909824492
5.5 x 8.5" Paperback
Published by Zaccmedia

FOCUSING BEYOND THE HORIZON
Samuel – Learning to see God's Perspective
Stephen Bishop

We relate to our surroundings by sight and sound. Together with our other senses we are able to interact with people and situations. But are these enough? Is more happening around us than we understand? Are we missing out on a further perspective?

This book, 'Focusing beyond the horizon,' looks at the Biblical character of Samuel in the Old Testament. Described as a prophet, or "seer", he saw more than the material world around him, being enabled to understand something of God's bigger picture.

Looking at the way in which God worked in Samuel's life, each bite-sized chapter in this material explores some of these factors and how we can also understand our world from God's viewpoint.

ISBN 9781909824737
5.5 x 8.5" Paperback
Published by Zaccmedia

Lightning Source UK Ltd.
Milton Keynes UK
UKOW06f0209040616

275581UK00001B/73/P